This Bible study is a warm and gentle welcome into the presence of God through small, daily disciplines which add up to large, lifetime results. Elizabeth invites us not to do more and try harder, but to reframe and rethink our daily habits. Like a big sister in the faith, she shares her own stories and experience, leads us through Scripture, and offers us practical encouragement to live each day in the presence of our kind and gentle Savior, who wants to tend to us. This study encouraged me, and I will be passing it on to the women in my church who want to grow in grace.

Jen Oshman, author, speaker, and women's ministry leader

Gently Tended is the reoriented approach to spiritual disciplines we need. Rather than looking at these disciplines as something more to do to be a "good Christian," Elizabeth encourages us through these practices to see more of who Christ is and what he has done. Her gentle teaching leads us not to more work, but to rest!

Kristen Hatton, LPC, author of *Parenting Ahead*

The challenge of talking about spiritual disciplines is that most Christians are reminded of things they know they should be doing—but aren't. These conversations lead many people to feelings of shame, and to white-knuckled effort to simply try harder and do better. In *Gently Tended,* Santelmann has offered a gospel-soaked and accessible approach to Christian formation. This book is a great resource for both personal use and group discussion.

Chad Kincer, teaching pastor at Frontline Church in Oklahoma City

During seasons of overwhelm or exhaustion, habits like Bible reading and prayer can feel burdensome. In *Gently Tended,* Elizabeth Santelmann tenderly invites us to set aside the guilt of "not doing enough" and to receive God's love right where we are. She offers practical, accessible guidance for gentle spiritual disciplines that help us draw near to God even in the midst of chaos.

Joanna Kimbrel, MATS, author and coordinator of women's initiatives for The Gospel Coalition

Gently Tended is an accessible and engaging Bible study on both the private and corporate expressions of some of the most overlooked spiritual disciplines that benefit and bless the church. Elizabeth's words are framed with delight rather than duty, with the aim of helping the reader towards living daily their chief end: glorifying and enjoying God forever.

Karen Hodge, coordinator of Women's Ministries for the Presbyterian Church in America (PCA) and author of *Transformed: Life-taker to Life-giver* and *Life-giving Leadership*

Gently Tended is a grace-filled journey through twelve essential spiritual practices—free from guilt or pressure. Elizabeth walks alongside you with the Scripture-saturated teaching, gentle guidance, and steady encouragement of a trusted mentor. Whether you've fallen out of the habit of regular Scripture intake or are longing to grow deeper in your walk with Christ, this book offers a faithful, approachable path forward—one that meets you where you are and helps you tend what truly matters.

Katie Orr, author of the FOCUSed15™ Bible study series and hostess of the Bible Study Hub™

Elizabeth's genuine care for her readers comes through in this astute yet gentle guide through these spiritual practices. With interactive reflections, rewarding opportunities to dig deeper into the Bible, and winsome devotional writing, this study is one I'll recommend to the women around me.

Felicity Carswell, cohost of Two Sisters and a Cup of Tea podcast and Bible teacher

Gently Tended is a warm invitation to explore the spiritual disciplines that God, in his grace, has given us as a means to grow in our love and knowledge of him and to become more like him. This study will exhort the reader to pursue spiritual disciplines not to earn God's love, but because they are greatly loved by him already. This study will help the reader turn ordinary minutes of each day into treasured moments with God.

Courtney Tracy, author of *Putting Jesus First: A 21-day Devotional Journey through Colossians*

As evangelicals, we love to talk about how we are shaped by the Bible. Yet often we neglect to see how formation must be joined to information, and how weekly worship forms us alongside one another. Enter Elizabeth Santelmann's *Gently Tended,* a rich resource for those in seasons of overwhelm. In the book, Santelmann reminds us of the primacy of God's Word, the shaping power of our covenant-keeping God, and practical steps to get biblical truths through our harried souls. How I wish I'd had Elizabeth Santelmann's book as a young mom. May it nourish and shape us toward theologically deep, biblically rich, and practically applicable lives of faith—in our homes and workplaces—for the good of the church.

Ashley Hales, editorial director at *Christianity Today,* cofounder of the Willowbrae Institute, and author of *A Fruitful Life, A Spacious Life,* and *Finding Holy in the Suburbs*

In *Gently Tended,* Elizabeth Santelmann holds open the front door to spiritual disciplines and warmly says, "Come on in!" This accessible, helpful study welcomes believers of all seasons to walk more closely with Jesus. Elizabeth's tender guidance offers needed ministry in a chaotic world, and I think it will especially bless the overwhelmed and anxious. (Ask me how I know!)

Caroline Saunders, author of *Come Home: Tracing God's Promise of Home Through Scripture*

Elizabeth writes with the same humility, grace, and Scripture-centered focus that mark her life and ministry. In *Gently Tended,* she invites weary believers to offer God their little and trust him to multiply it, consistently pointing readers to who God is rather than what they must do. Her words offer a gentle reprieve from performance-driven faith and a reminder of Jesus' tender care.

Asheritah Ciuciu, bestselling author of *Delighting in Jesus*

TYNDALE
MOMENTUM™

A Tyndale nonfiction imprint

Gently Tended

A Grace-Filled Bible Study for Practicing the Spiritual Disciplines

ELIZABETH SANTELMANN

Visit Tyndale online at tyndale.com.

Visit Elizabeth Santelmann at sunshineinmynest.com.

Visit tyndalechristianresources.com.

Gently Tended: A Grace-Filled Bible Study for Practicing the Spiritual Disciplines

Cover design by Julie Chen

Interior design by Laura Cruise

Published in association with the literary agency of Wolgemuth & Wilson.

For information about special discounts for bulk purchases, please contact Tyndale House Publishers at csresponse@tyndale.com, or call 1-855-277-9400.

ISBN 979-8-4005-1849-2

Printed in China

32 31 30 29 28 27 26
7 6 5 4 3 2 1

To my husband, Joseph,
who has held my hand, wiped my tears, and
spurred me on into deeper faith.

Contents

Foreword

As Elizabeth's friend, I want you to know something before you begin this study: She wrote it the same way she lives it—with sincerity, compassion, and a deep trust that God isn't intimidated by our limitations. I've watched her walk through seasons when life felt loud and demanding, when capacity was spread thin, and when the spiritual "ideal" felt out of reach. And yet I've also watched her learn how to notice God in ordinary moments, to return to him without shame, and to let simple practices become steady ground. This book isn't asking you to try harder; it's inviting you into a deeper faith. That's what makes *Gently Tended* such a gift.

There's a unique discouragement that can settle in when you love God and want to grow, but you're overwhelmed at the thought of how. You want deeper roots. You want to become someone who lives anchored in the Word, someone who's formed by Jesus in a way that changes your inner world, but your days already feel full, your mind feels crowded, and your energy is limited. Sometimes spiritual growth can feel like it belongs to people with more margin than you've got. Most of the women I know aren't lacking desire . . . they're lacking capacity.

Life is full of school drop-offs and deadlines. An invisible mental load and decision fatigue. Sleep deprivation and chronic stress. Grief that catches you off guard. Trying to keep everyone alive and cared for while quietly wondering where your own peace went in the process. In the busy seasons of life, even good things can start to feel heavy. Even spiritual disciplines can feel like pressure.

And that's why Elizabeth refuses to let tending to your spiritual life become one more task to check off the list. *Gently Tended* doesn't turn formation into performance. It doesn't make you feel behind. It doesn't offer another standard you can't keep and call it holiness. Instead, it offers something quieter and far more powerful: a gentle invitation back to the heart of God, the one who understands human limitation and meets it with compassion.

Throughout this study, Elizabeth reminds us that spiritual disciplines aren't a way to earn God's love. They're practices of presence. They're ordinary acts of obedience, faithful rhythms that help us become more aware of God's nearness in the middle of everyday life. They're not about proving ourselves. They're about being formed, slowly and honestly, by a God who's already close.

I truly love how practical this study is in showing how to start small. Not because small is trendy or cute, but because small is honest and applicable. A verse on a sticky note. A breath prayer in the carpool line. Gratitude on a hard day. A moment of silence before you pick up your phone. Small choices to return to God, even if yesterday you had nothing left to give.

One of the most meaningful aspects of this study is Elizabeth's invitation to keep a record of God's gentle tending. That practice alone can change the way you see your life and God's presence within it. So often we interpret our exhaustion as God's absence, but when we slow down, we start catching glimpses of the goodness that's been holding us all along. That's what you'll find in these pages.

You'll find disciplines taught with warmth, wisdom, and biblical clarity. You'll find room to breathe. You'll find permission to start where you are, with what you have, and you'll find a steady reminder that God isn't disappointed in your humanity. Your limitations don't limit God's capacity at work within and through you.

You're not behind. You're being gently tended.

So take your time. Receive what nourishes you, leave what you can't carry yet, and trust that God's Word never returns empty. You don't have to try harder. Today is a great day to try gentler.

Cassandra Speer
bestselling author, pediatric chaplain, podcast host,
and vice president of Her True Worth

Introduction

I spent my teens and early twenties working in children's ministry. As director of an after-school program, I poured my time and energy into caring for and discipling young kids in underserved communities. I read the Bible daily and was committed to memorizing Scripture and rigorously practicing spiritual disciplines like prayer and service.

Then I had my first baby.

Brain fog rested on me like a weight, making conversation with my family difficult and understanding what I read even harder.

Tears dripped down my chin as I stared at a passage in my Bible. I tried to read the words, but by the time I finished the second verse I had to go back and reread the first one because I couldn't remember what it was about. *What was wrong with me?* Three verses in I heard the baby crying.

I slammed the Bible shut and scurried off.

One thing after another popped up until I fell into bed exhausted. I was terrified the baby would be awake all night. "You pray," I begged my husband. "God will listen to you. I don't know what to say." Then I cried all over again.

I was so ashamed that I didn't breathe a word of my experience to anyone. But a few months later a friend slipped a book of index cards into my hand and said, "I write my favorite verses on index cards; then when I'm too overwhelmed for quiet time, I read one."

I looked down at my hand feeling like I had just experienced the church equivalent of a drug deal. *Could it be that easy? Did that count? Would God bless reading just one verse a day?*

Though I had lingering doubts, I decided to follow my friend's advice. At first I struggled to think of verses, but over the next few years they came to me more easily, and I jotted them down in my little book. By the time our next baby was born, the notebook was full. Sometimes I pulled it out and read as I nursed. Other times I copied verses onto separate cards and taped them up around the house.

I knew these small acts of fixing my eyes on Christ were growing my awareness of his presence, but deep down there was a nagging doubt. *Was this enough, or was I just placating myself into thinking I was doing enough because I wanted it to be true?*

Not long after, I was reading a passage from *Life Together* by theologian and martyr Dietrich Bonhoeffer, who recommended reflecting on small portions of Scripture during personal Bible study. He described how focusing on one verse for a week was potentially more transformative than scattered attention to many passages.[1] Joy swelled in my heart as I realized that what had been spiritually nourishing me was an acknowledged practice by someone I really respected.

That week, each time I settled into my nursing chair, I felt a renewed sense of purpose and energy as I looked at my little verse card and was reminded of God's truth and promises for my life.

By focusing my attention on one verse, I started noticing God's truth in other places. More verses came to my mind throughout the day, and particular lines from worship songs stood out to me. I was so transformed by this practice that, years later, I started making little note-card books of verses for friends who were going through seasons of life that felt impossible.

I began seeing God's promise in Isaiah 55:11 come to life: "So my word that comes from my mouth will not return to me empty, but it will accomplish what I please and will prosper in what I send it to do."

Slowly, I came to realize that our spiritual life isn't something we grow separate from our ordinary tasks. Instead, it's the simple things we do to integrate spiritual disciplines into our everyday life, so that every moment is lived in his presence with an awareness that "in him we live and move and have our being" (Acts 17:28).

Little Moments Count

Perhaps you, too, long for something more in your spiritual life. You want to be a person of deep faith, the one with the marked-up Bible and an intentional prayer list. Your problem isn't a lack of desire to grow a deeper spiritual connection to God but rather overwhelm at when and how to do it in the middle of all the chaos that life brings.

When you come to faith in Christ, the Holy Spirit lives inside you and constantly pulls you to know and love God more deeply. As the psalmist wrote, "God, you are my God; I eagerly seek you. I thirst for you; my body faints for you in a land that is dry, desolate, and without water" (Psalm 63:1).

But the call to move beyond the surface can feel impossible when you already feel like you're drowning in everyday tasks. Do you want to do it? Of course! But where is the energy going to come from to make it happen? Jesus predicted with compassion that this would be the human experience when he said in Matthew 26:41, "The spirit is willing, but the flesh is weak."

In the best of times, you can scrape together all your good habits to live your "ideal spiritual life." But eventually you find yourself juggling demanding coursework at school; you face an overwhelming deadline at work; chronic illness descends; you give birth and are awake six out of eight hours in the night; or you are called to care for an aging parent or spouse. What then? How do you grow closer to Jesus when the bone-tired exhaustion of sleepless nights piles up?

God understands your frailties, and he has provided a way for you to know him deeply without leaving your everyday life. You may not have space right now to study an entire book of the Bible, commit to a prayer hour, or volunteer to lead a women's retreat, but you can start small. Every day has space for a short reflection on God's Word. The simple faith habits that invite God's presence into your every moment are known as spiritual disciplines. As you fold these into your everyday life, they will leave you feeling refreshed and transformed.

Gently Tended Through the Spiritual Disciplines

I've put together this study to equip you with spiritual practices for growing closer to Christ, but in a way that takes little sit-down-and-focus time. The following sessions offer brief Scripture reflections—just a verse or two—on twelve spiritual disciplines. The spiritual disciplines are intentional, habitual practices that are explicitly taught in the Bible as ways believers can grow into mature faith. They are not ways to make God love you more, but rather ways you can cultivate an awareness of his love and be formed to be more like him.

Often when the spiritual disciplines are taught, they are presented in their most exaggerated forms, leading us to believe that God can only be reached through exhaustive efforts and long hours dedicated to quiet time and Scripture reading. I would like to use this study to show you the gentle love of your Father, who says he is so close that we live in his shadow (Psalm 91:1). You don't need to work hard to access his presence; he is already with you. Together, we will discover how to turn everyday moments into meaningful time with God.

Maybe these disciplines are something you work on a little every day or a little every week. Even if you pause or fall out of the habit for a few days (or weeks), he is always there, ready and waiting for you to pick it up again. You don't have to practice perfectly in order to see growth and experience transformation. Every moment given to God will bear spiritual fruit.

As you flip through these pages or scan the table of contents, you may see practices your pastor or tradition teaches, or you may see some that are less familiar. You may notice that some disciplines you've been taught are missing. I've included these twelve because they seem like the gentlest way to start, and they are the twelve I have the most experience with in my own walk with God. I believe I can only teach from what God has already taught me, and these are the ones he's used to draw me closer to him.

As you read and study, some of these disciplines may feel gentle to you—pick those up! If others feel overwhelming, make a little mental note and save those for when you have more margin. You will be shocked at what can happen in your heart by simply exposing yourself to an idea.

If you're studying alone and see a discipline that you've always wanted to know more about, feel free to jump to the one that you're curious about or that you most need. Chasing interest is a great way to build excitement and grow your love for learning!

No matter where you begin, remember that this is enough for this season. Focusing on one Scripture verse and discipline at a time doesn't mean you'll never read through the Bible in a year. It doesn't mean you're shallow. God's Word always accomplishes its purpose, so you can trust that any time you spend focusing on his Word and promises will be formative for you!

How to Use This Study

Before you get started, I've included some guidelines that will help you get the most out of this Bible study.

Individual and Group Study

This study can be completed individually or with a group. Maybe you're the kind of person who gets excited about something and then wants someone to share it with. If that's you, invite a friend or two to work through this study alongside you so you can encourage each other and be excited together as you learn. You might consider meeting at a home or coffee shop, or even gathering virtually through voice or video chat.

Maybe you're feeling shy about doing a Bible study with others and you want the freedom to go at your own pace. This study was written for you too! I will guide you through each session as we learn about the spiritual disciplines together.

If you're doing this study with a group, you'll want to watch the video teaching and complete the discussion questions during your group's scheduled meeting time. All other sections of the session are designed to be completed individually prior to your meeting so that you can focus your group time on discussion. (Though please feel free to adapt this structure to best meet the needs of your group.) Each group should have a leader who starts the video, keeps track of time, leads the group through the questions, and helps create a safe environment for participants to share their thoughts. For more guidance, see the Leader's Guide on page 205.

What You'll Need

You'll want to make sure you have a Bible on hand. The verses in this study are taken from the Christian Standard Bible (CSB) translation, but you are invited to bring your favorite Bible translation to this study. I find that using another translation can be fun because it provides fresh phrasing and perspective to reflect on the same truths of Scripture.

You'll also need a pen, maybe some markers, and a stack of index cards or Post-its to write the focus verse from each session. Feel free to make this as simple or creative as you like.

Lastly, you'll need access to a streaming device to watch the short video teachings that accompany each session.

What to Expect in Each Session

Video Teaching: At the front of your Bible study book, you'll find instructions on how to access the video teachings. I have recorded twelve videos introducing you to each discipline. Take some time to watch these with your group or listen on your own while you fold laundry, load the dishwasher, or put on your makeup. *My hope is that by hearing my voice you will feel the gentleness of these practices even more deeply.* Feel free to jot down notes in the "Session Notes" space provided if you find that helpful.

Discussion and Reflection Questions: If you're doing this study with a group, here is where you can connect and share your thoughts with other group members. If you're working through this study on your own, take a few moments for personal reflection as you read through each question.

A Record of God's Gentle Tending: It may feel like God is far away at times, but he is always present and at work in our lives—we just have to pause and notice. Take a little time with each discipline to keep a record of how God is gently tending you. Even if you never look at this study again, the act of writing down God's goodness to you will allow you to better see and remember the work he is doing.

Finding the Spiritual Disciplines in the Word: Each study focuses on a short verse or passage of Scripture that teaches you about a spiritual discipline. Write out these focus verses on index cards or Post-its, then hang them somewhere you'll see regularly. You can either read your verses as you see them or attempt to memorize them. The simple act of writing each verse will help solidify the Word of God in your memory. (If you want something cuter and more creative, you can visit sunshineinmynest.com/product/gently-tended and download free copies of hand-painted verse cards to print and write your verses on.)

After writing down your verse, you'll answer some tried-and-true study questions about that verse. In this Bible study, I draw from the inductive Bible study method, which aims to answer the following three questions of Scripture: What does it say? What does it mean? What does it mean for my life? In this section, we will focus on answering the first two questions.

Let's Dig In: It can be hard, even impossible, to dig into commentaries or source texts while living in seasons of overwhelm. Here, I've dug in a bit for you, providing easy-to-digest, "stuff you should know" sections, as well as personal stories, which will give you an even deeper appreciation of each session's focus verse and the work God has done both on the cross and in your own life.

In Context: If you're feeling spunky, I've included some additional Scripture verses that will help you see how the focus verse and teaching fit into the whole of Scripture and provide a fuller understanding of God's character and the calling he's given you. Don't feel pressured to get this done before your group meets. If your season changes and you feel up for it later, you can circle back. Or, if time allows, as a group, you can take turns looking up, reading, and reflecting on these verses together.

A Gentle Invitation into the Spiritual Disciplines: The final step of an inductive study is answering the question, What does this mean for my life? As we learn about Jesus, his work on the cross, and his calling on our lives, it inspires us to be transformed. This isn't a spot for you to beat yourself up but rather to gently consider the hope his work brings to your life today.

Prayer: At the end of each session, I've included a prayer for you to take into your week. I know there are times when I'm overwhelmed about what to pray. I wish I were there to take your hands and pray with you if you're feeling that way too. These prayers are the closest I can get to doing that, and I hope they are an encouragement to you.

If you got really into the session's topic and have bonus time, I've included a few extra sections for further study:

Digging Deeper into the Spiritual Disciplines

A Second Look

Additional Context

A Second Invitation into the Spiritual Disciplines

In these sections, you'll find an additional focus verse, commentary, and context section, as well as another opportunity to apply the session's discipline to your life. *Important note*: If you leave these final sections blank, or complete them for some lessons but not others, *you have not failed this study!* You may find that a week, month, or year later you want to come back and dig into an idea a little more. It will be here waiting for you!

Please be gentle with yourself. Take what is encouraging to you and trust that God's Word doesn't return empty. He will nourish you with as much or as little as you have capacity for today and lead you back to it when you're ready.

A Final Note

I'm so honored that you are allowing me to walk with you to our heavenly Father who gently tends us. Someday when I see you face-to-face, I can't wait to tell you about how he did that for me while I wrote this book, and I hope you can tell me about how he met you in these pages as well.

Gently Tending

Your Heart and Mind

You have immediate adoption into God's family at the moment of salvation. Now you can live free and in relationship with God as your Father. You get to know him on a more personal basis by listening to the stories he tells about himself, having conversations with him, and seeing the way he is faithful to meet your needs when you trust him. The spiritual disciplines in this section will invite you to know God personally. This knowledge isn't just information that stays in your head, but rather truth that equips you to be more like him and transforms your heart, mind, and life.

Bible Study

The term *Bible study* may conjure up images of Instagram posts with coffee, candles, highlighters, and an open Bible—the perfect setup for long, quiet hours of reading chapter after chapter. But this is vastly different from the way the early church studied God's Word. For the first one thousand years after Christ, most people didn't have personal copies of the Bible. They would read it together corporately, discuss it, and mull over what they had heard throughout their week.

Bible study is the practice of exposing ourselves to what the Bible says and applying those truths to our lives. So read or listen to what you can retain, and seek to deepen your understanding of the meaning. The goal is for his Word to be a major forming influence in your life.

Video Notes

DISCUSSION AND REFLECTION QUESTIONS

- Can you remember a time in your life when you studied your Bible often? What made it meaningful, and how did you grow through it?
- What resources do you use to help you study the Bible? Have you used them recently?
- What is a Bible verse that is particularly meaningful to you, and why is it important? If you're working in a group, write your favorite verse on an index card and exchange cards with one another.

To access the video session, use the instructions in the front of your Bible study book.

A Record of God's Gentle Tending

Sometimes we think God doesn't meet with us, when really we just don't pause long enough to notice what he's already doing. Take a moment to record how God is tending you.

Look back over your life. What are some ways God has used the Bible to show himself to you? Is there a passage from Scripture he's recently used to transform one part of your life? Describe that experience.

Finding Bible Study in the Word

Write out Romans 12:2 on an index card or Post-it so you can refer to it throughout your week.

Now let's take some time to look deeply at Romans 12:2. We want to see this verse in its context, understand the words used, and discover its meaning.

What do you think are the key words in this verse?

Do not be conformed to this age, but be transformed by the renewing of your mind, so that you may discern what is the good, pleasing, and perfect will of God.

ROMANS 12:2

Look up the words *conformed* and *transformed* in the dictionary, then write this verse in your own words.

What is the result of having our minds transformed by truth?

LET'S DIG INTO

Bible Study

The other day I was telling a friend that one of the most formative influences in my life has been who I married. My husband and I have been married thirteen years. We've talked so much that we know nearly all each other's stories from childhood, teen years, and young adulthood. Though occasionally he will tell a story that, much to my delight, surprises me.

I've found that the more I know about my husband, the dearer he becomes to me. I understand his motivations and the choices he makes. Our conversations have helped shape who I am, what my interests are, and the way I talk to people. His tenderness has helped me become less self-critical and more confident about trying new things.

Reading God's Word does something similar to us. Bible teacher Jen Wilkin often says, "The heart cannot love what the mind does not know."[2] Without spending time with God, it's possible to be vaguely spiritual. But to really love God, we must get to know him. He's made that possible by giving us hundreds of pages of stories and teachings about who he is. In his Word, we also learn how much he loves us and that he has intimately known us since before we were even born (Psalm 139:13-14).

When we read his Word and ask the deep, hard questions of our faith, we grow to know God more intimately and develop deep trust in him that cannot be shaken no matter how many years pass or what trials come.

In today's verse, Romans 12:2, Paul calls believers in Rome to stand firm in God's truth amid a pagan society. It's hard to imagine what the world was like before the widespread influence of Christian ethics, but let's try for a moment. In Roman culture, you married mainly for status and to have children who would help advance your business ventures. Though Romans rejoiced when a child was born to them, they did not consider children fully human until adulthood. Sometimes families left unwanted babies in the wilderness to die of exposure. Other times these abandoned infants were adopted or taken to be raised as slaves or prostitutes. If you were in a financially tight place, you could sell your children for profit. Women were legally required to follow the demands of their husbands. And while some forms of Roman entertainment were peaceful—like poetry readings and theater performances—many others were brutal and violent. In the Colosseum, human life was only as valuable as the enjoyment it created. Crowds would watch as slaves or prisoners fought to the death. The gods they worshiped were unstable and manipulative.[3]

Into this world, Christians came to teach about a God who loves people so much that he sent his Son to die for them. While on earth, Jesus healed people, ate with them, and gathered children to himself. In Romans 12:2, Paul urges the early church not to be shaped by the city they lived in, but rather by the beautiful new truth they had found in Jesus.

We are all daily being formed by the things that we are continually exposed to—whether it's the speech patterns of our friends, jokes from the TV shows we watch, or the theology of our church family.

Less innocent types of formation come as we scroll social media and are told that our aging faces are a problem. We read novels that suggest we'd be happier with a husband who has a better personality. Advertisements try to convince us that anxiety can be masked with substances, and our fear of missing out can be cured by spending more money on experiences.

It can be tempting to listen to all these voices. But the goal of a Christian is to spend time studying the Word of God so that it is the major forming influence in our lives and gives us discernment to recognize the lies culture is selling.

When we think of "doing Bible study," we often picture quiet, personal time spent reading our Bibles. But this is much different from the way the early Christians studied God's Word. In the historical period when the New Testament was written, most people didn't even have personal copies of Scripture. Instead, they would gather to read it together, then discuss and reflect on it in the days that followed. God's Word was integrated into their daily rhythms.

We are transformed by the renewing of our minds (Romans 12:2). But our minds can only be transformed if we are exposing them to things that are true, lovely, and commendable (Philippians 4:8). When we follow the pattern of calling on the Lord, believing in him, and discussing and sharing his Word (Romans 10:14-15), it causes us to be transformed.

If you're like me, you grab your phone off your nightstand first thing in the morning. You settle down in the evening with another quick scroll. You burn through page after page in your novel while the Bible study lies dusty on the desk. Or you hop from social event to social event without pausing to think about how it went and how the experience impacted you.

We know we can't form ourselves. We've tried, and we've come up lacking. Jesus is the perfect Son of God who sacrificed himself to save us from our own shortcomings, and because of him we can have an intimate relationship with God and be blessed as we are formed by his Word.

We can rest in the truths laid out in his Word, knowing that even if we don't immediately understand everything, he is good, and his ways are good. We don't have to see aging as a problem, but can find peace in the truth that aging brings wisdom acquired from years of being formed by the gospel and ushers us into God's presence when this life passes. God's Word shows us how marriage and family life give us the space to humble ourselves and serve. His truth enables us to remove ourselves from the center of the universe and practice the disciplines of our faith in daily life.

But how can we do this if we don't know what the Word says? The goal of our reading isn't to "get through" but to remember and apply. If reading God's Word isn't bringing delight, blessing, and transformation, then maybe we're approaching it the wrong way. Perhaps we've begun treating it like a competition to read the most, just to feel good about ourselves. Or on the flip side, maybe it's become something unnecessary to our existence.

We can reclaim our joy in Bible study when we trust that God is using it to gently tend to our souls. He promises that his Word will not return empty (Isaiah 55:11). So read what you have brain retention for and take small steps to incorporate his truths into your daily rhythms. Maybe that looks like sticking a verse on your bathroom mirror, changing the station from music that glamorizes sin to music that leads to worship, or surrounding yourself with other faithful women and digging into the Word together. Slowly, you will notice that you are being formed by the one who refused to be conformed by the world.

In Context

I've listed some of my favorite passages on Bible study below. After reading each passage in your Bible, use the space provided to respond to one (or both) of these questions:

What does this teach you about how and why to study the Bible?

What does this reveal to you about who God is?

You can also choose to simply write out the passage. Writing the Word of God helps solidify it in our hearts.

Psalm 119:11

Psalm 119:105

Hebrews 4:12

2 Timothy 3:16-17

A Gentle Invitation into Bible Study

What do you need most in life to start reading God's Word more regularly—to lock in on really hearing what the Bible is saying and applying its truths to your life?

What have you learned today that shows you who God is?

Prayer

Father, thank you for wanting a relationship with your people so much that you created a way for us to know you intimately.

Help me not to use your Word as a weapon to beat myself up when I fail, but to understand your grace and your love for me! Teach me to know you better this week.

Digging Deeper into Bible Study

If you have bonus time, I invite you to explore an additional verse on Bible study. Write out Isaiah 55:11 on an index card or Post-it so you can refer to it throughout your week.

Now let's take some time to look deeply at Isaiah 55:11. We want to see this verse in its context, understand the words used, and discover its meaning.

What is the promise of this verse?

So my word that comes from my mouth will not return to me empty, but it will accomplish what I please and will prosper in what I send it to do.

ISAIAH 55:11

When we look at Isaiah 55, what clues show that verse 11 is a promise, not a threat?

Isaiah was prophesying to God's covenant people who had become corrupt and rejected him. In the book, we see the narrative arc of coming judgment, a promised Messiah, and the compassion of God. How might that context make the promise of this verse even more meaningful and tangible?

A SECOND LOOK AT

Bible Study

The smell of grass floated in through the open window of our farmhouse. The pulse of the buzzing cicadas made it seem as if the air was breathing. I lay sprawled out across my twin bed, so engrossed in my book that I hardly noticed the sticky July heat. A tear slowly slid down my face as I turned a page.

Every paragraph of the missionary testimony I was reading was laced with Scripture. Miracle after miracle unfolded as the chapters slipped by. Newlywed Darlene Deibler Rose went to a mission field in New Guinea to serve alongside several elderly missionaries right before the start of World War II.

When news of the war reached them, their whole group prayed to see if they should leave or stay. Unanimously they decided to stay, and a short time later they received word that the ship they would have left on was torpedoed three days after it set sail. There were no survivors.

Eventually, the Japanese military took control of the region where Darlene and her husband were serving, and they were imprisoned in different camps. Accused of being a spy, Darlene was put in a maximum-security prison where, upon arrival, the commander took her Bible. She said in her testimony, "He didn't know that as a little girl I went to bed every night with this book [my Bible] in front of me. And I began to memorize it, and I started in with Genesis. There was much of this book that was there on the grooves of my mind for the Holy Spirit just to drop the needle down on it and play it back to me. So I didn't mind him taking my Bible."[4]

Day after day, year after year, God sustained her through the verses she had memorized. Time and time again he answered her prayers, and she was comforted in her grief.

The words of God that Darlene had memorized as a child didn't just sit in her mind or run through her thoughts as a mantra. They transformed who she was and the way she reacted to the pain and struggle that life brought her way.

Similarly, God encouraged Israel through the prophet Isaiah. Israel had been a wandering people, and they were given the law of God to guide their faith and a place to settle down in the land God had promised Abraham. For a while they had God as their ultimate King, and judges who helped to deliver them. But eventually Israel wanted an earthly king so they could be like the nations around them. While King David and his son Solomon taught Israel to love God more and made a place for them to worship, after a few decades, their earthly kings led them into idol worship and poverty. The Scriptures were lost, and worship of God mostly stopped.

Isaiah was a prophet during this phase of Israel's history. He warned that they would be taken captive and punished unless they repented of their sin and turned to God. He encouraged them to listen to Scripture and obey it. And he told them of God's promise of restoration, even in the face of punishment and exile. In today's verse, Isaiah 55:11, God is speaking through Isaiah to remind Israel that they can trust in his promises.

We, too, can place our trust in God's Word. The purpose of studying the Bible isn't to become stuffed with knowledge but rather to be transformed by his Spirit (Romans 12:2). We are putting off our old ways and putting on the new way of life God has given us (Ephesians 4:22-24). Just like Darlene Deibler Rose and the Israelites, we are invited to lean into God's Word to sustain and guide us each day, no matter what comes our way.

When we read the Word with an open heart, ready to do what it says, God transforms the way we see the world. His attitudes start to become our attitudes. What breaks his heart breaks ours, and what brings him joy brings us joy.

Studying the Word brings joy because it reminds us that God hasn't handed us over to the influence of a broken world. He lays out his heart in a way that we can access and walks beside us as we become more like him. I had a mentor tell me once that someone can show up to therapy for years and make no progress until it finally "clicks" and they see how they need to change. That, for them, is day one. The same thing happens in the life of a believer. We can believe in Jesus and be saved, knowing that grace covers us and we are his children. However, there is a different kind of transformation that happens when a Christian dedicates themself to the study of God's Word.

We don't study the Bible to earn our salvation—Jesus already paid that price. Rather, when we open our Bibles, we are accepting Jesus' gentle invitation to walk with him and become more like him: "Take my yoke upon you and learn from me. . . . For my yoke is easy and my burden is light" (Matthew 11:29-30). Bible study *does* require effort and intentionality—Jesus describes following him as wearing a "yoke." Yokes for ancient people were always connected to work. But he also promises that his yoke is "easy," meant to lead us into freedom and flourishing.

The Bible is God's path for us to find flourishing in the world he created. Of course, because we live in a broken world, we can never find complete fulfillment here. When the first humans sinned, the ground became cursed and pain and death entered in.

Yet the joy we have as Christians is knowing that when things became broken, God didn't leave us. Jesus came to be perfect for us. He endured a crown of thorns on our behalf. He was publicly mocked. His flesh was torn. Then he died to make things new again. Even though the earth is still groaning under the effects of sin, we are told of a Kingdom to come with no more tears. The peace we experience in Christ now is just a shadow of what is to come. The more we dig into his Word, the more real it becomes to us. And when we live in alignment with the ways of the new Kingdom, we play a part in pointing others to the glory that is to come!

It's easy to come to Bible study with fear that we will get it wrong. Or maybe someone misled us into believing that we *should* be doing it a particular way. But we can rest in the truth that, like our verse says, God's Word does not return empty but accomplishes its purpose. The true goal of reading the Word of God is to love Jesus, know him more, and be transformed to become more like him. It is tapping into Jesus, the True Vine, who enables us to produce good fruit in our lives. As we learn more about the study of God's Word, let's move into it with joy and the hope of transformation.

Additional Context

I've listed some more of my favorite passages on Bible study below. After reading each passage in your Bible, use the space provided to respond to one (or both) of these questions:

What does this teach you about how and why to study the Bible?

What does this reveal to you about who God is?

You can also choose to simply write out the passage. Writing the Word of God helps solidify it in our hearts.

1 Peter 2:2

Proverbs 30:5

Isaiah 40:8

Psalm 119:18

A Second Invitation into Bible Study

Sometimes embracing new spiritual practices can feel hard. What, if anything, about Bible study makes you uncomfortable? Take a moment to pray over your concerns, remembering that Jesus meets each one with gentleness and compassion.

How does what you've read change the way you feel called to live?

Prayer

Prayer is not just public speaking to God or saying the "right" words to unlock the power of God. Prayer is more about faith and remembering that the Holy Spirit lives in you and communicates with you. You are invited into divine fellowship with God!

Video Notes

DISCUSSION AND REFLECTION QUESTIONS

- What is prayer? Do you know anyone whose prayers or prayer life encourages you?
- Can you think of a specific time when God answered your prayers?
- Have you ever prayed and felt like it just bounced off the ceiling?

To access the video session, use the instructions in the front of your Bible study book.

A Record of God's Gentle Tending

Sometimes we think God doesn't meet with us, when really we just don't pause long enough to notice what he's already doing. Take a moment to record how God is tending you.

Record a time you've seen God answer prayer in the past. How might his faithfulness to you in the past bring encouragement for what you're facing today?

Finding Prayer in the Word

Write out 1 Thessalonians 5:16-18 on an index card or Post-it so you can refer to it throughout your week.

Now let's take some time to look deeply at 1 Thessalonians 5:16-18. We want to see this passage in its context, understand the words used, and discover its meaning.

What three practices are part of God's will for us, according to this passage?

Look at this passage again and write it in your own words. (For help, you can read the passage in another Bible translation or consult a dictionary or thesaurus to better understand the words used.)

Rejoice always, pray constantly, give thanks in everything; for this is God's will for you in Christ Jesus.

1 THESSALONIANS 5:16-18

Can you think of an Old Testament story where someone prayed? How did God answer? (If you can't think of an example, see 1 Samuel 1:1-20.)

LET'S DIG INTO

Prayer

Ice crunched under the tires of the car as two friends pulled into our driveway. These men were skilled mechanics who had just joined our church and were new to faith. They needed a rototiller engine to put onto their log splitter, and my parents offered to let them borrow ours. I walked them to the garage, where they got the engine off the rototiller and tried for a long time to get it onto the log splitter. But it seemed like there was no logical way the two pieces would fit. Beads of sweat started to prickle on their foreheads from the effort.

Pained by their frustration, yet knowing any mechanical knowledge I had to contribute wouldn't be helpful, I asked them if we could pray before they tried again. They laughed uncomfortably, and one rolled his eyes, but we all bowed our heads to simply pray that God would help it work.

They again picked up the piece and pushed on it as hard as they could, slightly sarcastically as if to prove prayer didn't work like that. The piece immediately slid into place, and we all started laughing in disbelief. We knew that God answered prayer, but we'd never seen an example of him working so directly.

God doesn't always answer our prayers immediately or in the way we expect, as he did in this situation, but this experience reminded me that God does listen and wants us to bring every concern to him. After seeing a direct answer to prayer that day with the rototiller, I knew the power of prayer. Yet for years after that I struggled with guilt over not praying enough. In the chaos of life, I rarely had time to pray. And I definitely didn't pray as soon as I woke up or before I went to bed. For a long time, I thought about prayer only in terms of *stopping* to pray.

What I have learned since is that God doesn't want us to just come to him as a vending machine or in the big moments, but in the small ones. The breaths of prayer when we're struggling to control our temper. Exclamations of gratitude when we see something beautiful. Or a small prayer when remembering someone we love who is grieving or ill. These prayers in daily living help us to embody the Bible's instruction to "pray constantly" (1 Thessalonians 5:17).

First Thessalonians is one of the earliest letters written by Paul to a church. While teaching the church in Thessalonica, Paul had to make a hasty departure under the cover of darkness (Acts 17:10-11). He wanted to teach them everything he didn't have time to finish teaching when he was there, so he wrote to them. One of the key themes in his message, as seen in 1 Thessalonians 5:16-18, is the way prayer changed after Christ's death on the cross.

Prayer after Jesus died was radically different from the time before Jesus, when requests to God were made alongside a sacrifice at the Temple. There, a high priest would advocate on behalf of the people in the Holy of Holies, a curtained off area of the Temple that held the Ark of the Covenant. Atop the Ark was a lid called the mercy seat, where God's presence rested. But not everyone could go into the Holy of Holies. High priests were only allowed to enter once per year, and they had to perform purifying rituals before entering God's presence. Apart from that one day each year, prayers and sacrifices were only made in the outer courts of the Temple.

But the moment Jesus died, the curtain that separated the people from the Holy of Holies was miraculously torn from top to bottom. Jesus' death and resurrection brought us direct access to the throne of God.

Paul's letter to the Thessalonians shows us that many believers struggle with prayer. Like any habit, it's one we have to learn. But it's also an outpouring of our faith. That means we don't have to muster enough strength to do it ourselves. We can ask God to remind us to pray. Then God grows our faith as we continue to seek him and see evidence of his work in our lives. Romans 10:17 says, "Faith comes from what is heard, and what is heard comes through the message about Christ."

Your prayer life reveals what you truly believe about God. However, regardless of how "good" or "bad" you think you are at praying, you are God's beloved child. Prayer doesn't make him love you more, but it allows you to see who he is and the kindness he has for you.

We can easily fall into the trap of thinking that prayer is just public speaking to God. Then rather than being encouraged by the prayers of others, we use them as a basis for comparison, despair, and self-condemnation.

But God greets your prayers with the open loving arms of a father. He can and often does bless you without you making the request, just as a father meets the needs of little ones before they know to ask. But prayer is still important because it is part of your spiritual relationship with him. To truly understand prayer, you have to understand the watchful affection God has for you. This knowledge will cause you to run to him with your requests and pain.

You can come to God with faltering and imperfect words or without words at all because Jesus is interceding for you (Romans 8:26-27). If the Holy Spirit lives inside you, he will gently tend you in prayer. You don't have to make special time in your day for prayer. Prayer can be part of your thoughts throughout the day. So don't wait until you have the time for a long prayer or a complex written one. Bring prayer into the joy and pain of your daily life. The answers you see will deepen your faith and result in even more prayer.

In Context

I've listed some of my favorite passages on prayer below. After reading each passage in your Bible, use the space provided to respond to one (or both) of these questions:

What does this teach you about how and why to pray?

What does this reveal to you about who God is?

You can also choose to simply write out the passage. Writing the Word of God helps solidify it in our hearts.

Philippians 4:6-7

James 5:16

Matthew 6:5-8

Matthew 7:7-11

A Gentle Invitation into Prayer

What has the discipline of prayer taught you about God's character?

What about prayer makes you feel excited, curious, or overwhelmed?

Prayer

Lord, you are with me every second of every day. You know when I go to bed and when I get back up again. Help me to know you in such a way that my every thought revolves around you. Let me remember that you don't only meet me when I bow my head, close my eyes, or say "Dear Jesus," but that your compassion for me is intertwined in every moment of my life. I breathe in your love and breathe out my needs to you.

Digging Deeper into Prayer

If you have bonus time, I invite you to explore an additional passage on prayer. Write out Romans 8:26-27 on an index card or Post-it so you can refer to it throughout your week.

Now let's take some time to look deeply at Romans 8:26-27. We want to see this passage in its context, understand the words used, and discover its meaning.

In the same way the Spirit also helps us in our weakness, because we do not know what to pray for as we should, but the Spirit himself intercedes for us with inexpressible groanings. And he who searches our hearts knows the mind of the Spirit, because he intercedes for the saints according to the will of God.

ROMANS 8:26-27

Who are the key figures mentioned in this passage? What role do they each play?

What is the progression of prayer laid out in this passage? Can you fill in the diagram to show how our prayers are brought before God? Be sure to include God the Father, the believer, and the Holy Spirit in your drawing.

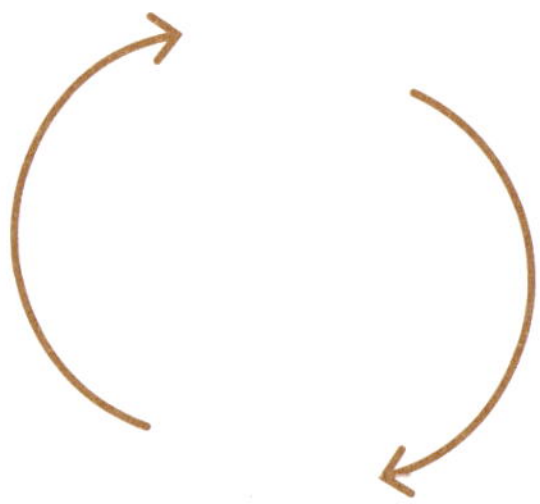

How do you think this understanding of prayer is different from what the Jews believed about prayer before Jesus?

A SECOND LOOK AT

Prayer

The first chapter book I ever read was the story of a missionary. That introduction caused me to fall in love with reading the stories of men and women of faith. A few years later my mom introduced me to a man who became known as Praying Hyde. I'm using the word *introduced* loosely, because by the time I learned about him, he had been dead nearly one hundred years. She drove us to a graveyard in the small town of Carthage, Illinois, where I was born. There, under the towering oak trees, was a tombstone that read "John N. Hyde." The back bore the inscription "Praying Hyde of India."

John Hyde was born in Illinois, but he felt called to serve in India. At age twenty-seven, he left everyone he knew to travel by boat across the Atlantic Ocean to the Punjab region of Northern India. John immediately ran into some problems. Because a childhood illness had left him partially deaf, learning a new language was significantly harder than he had anticipated. For years he labored to communicate and preach, but with very little fruit. The longer he lived in India, the less time he spent preaching and the more time he set aside to pray. By year seven he was spending entire nights in prayer.

Slowly, a prayer group gathered, and John felt led to pray that one person per day would come to know Christ. By the end of the year, God answered that prayer by bringing four hundred people to know him. In the following years John continued to increase his goal for conversions. More than any other part of what John did, prayer defined his ministry.[5] At forty-seven years old, he went to be with his Savior, but he left a legacy of prayer so strong that one hundred years later it sparked the imagination of another little girl from his hometown of Carthage.

While his story inspired me with a vision for what I wanted my prayer life to look like, it also led to confusion, guilt, and longing because I couldn't quite put it into practice. I struggled because many of my prayers seemed to go unanswered. To guard myself from disappointment, I slowly quit praying. For three years I served in kids' ministry and taught them to pray, and it felt like I was attempting to sell something I didn't really believe or live out for myself.

I was busy working for God without talking to him or engaging in meaningful relationship with him. That is, until I realized that prayer could look different from what I was imagining it to be.

Today's passage, Romans 8:26-27, assures us of the Spirit's help when we don't know what to pray for. It shows us that we have a kind, gentle, and compassionate Savior. Jesus knew prayer would be hard. While here on earth, he taught his disciples how to pray, providing a model Christians can still use today (Matthew 6:9-13), especially in times of confusion or when the words don't come naturally. God sympathizes with weakness in prayer. He cares about what we care for—so much so that he came to live as we live and experience the cares we have. Then he died and rose again to pay for our sins and sent the Holy Spirit to live inside us and comfort us.

It took me a long time to figure out that prayer can look many different ways. It isn't exclusively laying hands on something or someone and seeing instant results from the words that are said. Prayer isn't just kneeling by a bed, leaning over a Bible, or rewriting a psalm to God in my journal—all of which are great ways to pray, but they can often feel more like service to God than intimacy with God.

When I began meditating on Romans 8:26-27, I realized that what I was imagining prayer to be was closer to magic spells than closeness to God. I believed that if I just said all the "right" words, I could unlock the power of God and get the results I desired. In reality, prayer is about faith and remembering that the Holy Spirit lives in me, and his spirit communicates with my spirit (1 Corinthians 6:19).

I avoided prayer because it was always accompanied by guilt and shame. When I *did* remember to pray, all I could think about was how long it had been since I had last prayed. God wired our brains to engage in activities that bring joy, so when I began experiencing the peace that his presence brings and learned that I was cared for even when I didn't articulate my needs with words, it made me want to run to him more often.

In Romans 8:26-27, we read that the Spirit communicates with God in inexpressible groanings (other translations state that these are "too deep for words"). God is not bound by language. If the Holy Spirit lives in me, he can search my heart (Psalm 139:23-24). He doesn't need prayer to know what I'm thinking about. He knows what is in my mind whether I choose to speak it into a specific prayer or not. And the things that make me anxious touch his heart.

You may be like me, the kind of person who feels things deeply. I cry when I hear about someone else's pain, and then I think of them many times the rest of the week. What I didn't realize at first is that since the Holy Spirit lives in me, being moved in compassion for another was translated by him into prayer.

From then on, when someone told me something hard, I could earnestly say that I would be praying for them and mean it, because I knew I would think of their pain repeatedly. Since I had God's Spirit living inside of me, he would see and know how it affected me and bring it before the Father. This removed the guilt that I wasn't praying enough. Free from guilt, I slowly started to bring my concerns more intentionally in prayer to God.

From there, I noticed my anxiety decreasing. While I had no power to control the outcomes of someone's life, God had the power to write stories however he saw fit, and I could rest in the truth that he held everything in his loving hands. I also knew that I could "cry out 'Abba, Father!'" (Romans 8:15), and like a good father he would hear my anxiety and hold me through it.

Author and theologian Michael Reeves says it well: "Prayer, then, is not actually a one-way conversation, us to God. No, in prayer God speaks through us to God. We're brought into the divine fellowship. The Spirit of the Son cries to the Father through us."[6]

In those low times when I couldn't find the words to pray, I was comforted knowing that the Spirit himself was praying on my behalf.

God isn't shocked or ashamed that we are human. In fact, we see the opposite throughout the Bible. He came to earth to meet us where we are and cover our weakness in his perfection and strength. He's not surprised that we struggle to pray. He isn't waiting with arms crossed for us to *finally* come to him in prayer. His desire is to help his children. We don't have to fake it until we make it with him. He knows what's on our hearts, and he feels our concerns.

Additional Context

I've listed some more of my favorite passages on prayer below. After reading each passage in your Bible, use the space provided to respond to one (or both) of these questions:

What does this teach you about how and why to pray?

What does this reveal to you about who God is?

You can also choose to simply write out the passage. Writing the Word of God helps solidify it in our hearts.

Colossians 4:2

Mark 11:24

Matthew 6:9-13

Psalm 86:5-7

A Second Invitation into Prayer

Is there a particular aspect of prayer that you struggle with? Do you have any unanswered questions about prayer? Bring these concerns before God, and be on the lookout for how he responds in the coming week.

How would integrating prayer more deeply into your daily rhythms change the way you live?

Gratitude

Gratitude is remembering God's grace with joy.

It's not an invitation to repay or earn God's grace but to rejoice in what Jesus, the promised Savior, has already done—not just on the cross but in each day of our lives.

Practicing gratitude involves a heart change in which we recognize that we don't create the good in our own lives and that good things don't come to us by luck, attraction, or manifesting. All good things are given to us by God.

This remembrance makes us ready and willing to show appreciation by telling others of God's works and recording what he has done.

Video Notes

DISCUSSION AND REFLECTION QUESTIONS

- What are some simple gifts you're grateful for?
- Have you ever intentionally listed things you're grateful for? How did it change your perspective?
- How does gratitude intersect with faith?

To access the video session, use the instructions in the front of your Bible study book.

A Record of God's Gentle Tending

Sometimes we think God doesn't meet with us, when really we just don't pause long enough to notice what he's already doing. Take a moment to record how God is tending you.

What has been life-giving lately (the things that have made your body feel light)? Write about someone God has used to encourage you.

Finding Gratitude in the Word

Write out Colossians 3:16 on an index card or Post-it so you can refer to it throughout your week.

Now let's take some time to look deeply at Colossians 3:16. We want to see this verse in its context, understand the words used, and discover its meaning.

What are the Christian practices listed in this verse?

Let the word of Christ dwell richly among you, in all wisdom teaching and admonishing one another through psalms, hymns, and spiritual songs, singing to God with gratitude in your hearts.

COLOSSIANS 3:16

According to this verse, what inspires these Christian practices? What is the source from which they flow?

Can you think of someone from Scripture who expressed gratitude to God? Describe their story and how they offered thanks. (If you can't think of an example, see Luke 17:11-19.)

LET'S DIG INTO

Gratitude

I used to come to Communion with a heavy heart. I saw it as a time to recite all my failures so I could feel properly guilty and muster up the desire to change. But a few years ago, I learned that the word *Communion,* commonly used in church services, is interchangeable with the traditional word *Eucharist.* The definition of the word *Eucharist* stopped me in my tracks and transformed the way I interacted with that part of the service on Sundays.

Eucharist, in essence, means to be thankful for grace with joy.[7] When we take Communion/Eucharist at church on Sunday, it's a space carved into our week to be grateful. The table of the Lord isn't a place to commit to try harder but to rejoice in what Jesus, our Savior, has done—not just on the cross but in each day of our lives.

I've come to take that practice of worship a step further, remembering not just what he has done but also what he has promised to do. Every week something comes up that breaks my heart and reminds me that this world isn't my home. I use a portion of the Communion time to remember that he has promised to bring his Kingdom and make all things new.

Just like I used to add to the gospel by making myself feel guilty during Communion, the church in Colossae was also adding things to the gospel. They were attempting to become "more holy" by giving up certain foods and drinks and by following legalistic practices based on Old Testament law. Paul wrote to this little town, even though he had never visited it, to encourage the people to keep the teachings of Jesus at the center of their lives and remember the work he had done for them on the cross. By relying on their own efforts to become right with God, they were robbing themselves of the opportunity to receive God's grace and live joyfully with grateful hearts.

I fell into the same trap as the Colossians when I attempted to observe Communion "properly." I thought that by serving well or performing perfectly I could become a better Christian. I believed that through self-denial and self-condemnation I could be more deserving of forgiveness.

This can also look like responding to an altar call every time it's offered, attempting to repent "fervently enough," volunteering for every church activity, or tamping down feelings of guilt for spiritual shortcomings by purchasing a theological library one Amazon box at a time.

None of these things make us better or more holy, and they cannot make us right with God. The work Christ did on our behalf is completely sufficient for our salvation. We have had all our failures fully paid for by him, and he gives us his Spirit to live inside us and draw us toward him. He is the one who transforms us. There is nothing we can inflict on our bodies or squeeze out of our lives to make this change. We were dead, and he made us alive. He took our debt and nailed it to the cross.

This helps us better understand the meaning of today's focus verse, Colossians 3:16. When Paul says to admonish "one another through psalms, hymns, and spiritual songs, singing to God with gratitude in your hearts," he isn't describing how to be "more saved" but rather how to be formed by the gospel. Paul tells us what being formed by the gospel is going to look like. It's going to lead to a life marked by compassion, kindness, humility, gentleness, patience, and forgiveness (see Colossians 3:12-13). Notice how that sounds like the fruit of the Spirit in Galatians 5? The transformation that happens when the Holy Spirit is inside us will have a predictable effect. But we can only experience this transformation and be led into gratitude when we consistently remember the work that Christ has done.

In the Old Testament, the people of Israel remembered God's faithfulness by setting up memorial stones in places where God had intervened and helped them. In 1 Samuel 7, we read of the prophet Samuel setting up a stone called "Ebenezer" after God gave the Israelites victory over the Philistines. It's important to note that setting up these stones didn't force God's hand to work; he'd already rescued them. The stones simply served as reminders of God's faithfulness.

Every time they walked by, they would see the stones and remember what God had done. This prompted them not only to give thanks but also to tell the story to their kids, allowing them to put into practice the principle given in Deuteronomy 6:7: "Repeat [God's commands] to your children. Talk about them when you sit in your house and when you walk along the road, when you lie down and when you get up."

Recounting God's goodness builds faith, helps us move toward life change, and stirs gratitude in our hearts. Maybe you know the old hymn that says, "Count your many blessings, name them one by one, and it will surprise you what the Lord hath done."[8] An easy way to invite God to gently tend our souls is to start recording what he has done. Sometimes we forget everything he's done until we start recording it.

In Colossians 3:16, Paul gives us a template for remembering God's faithfulness: Let God's Word dwell in us as we teach one another. When someone isn't speaking truth, nurture the tending of their soul by listening, but then also gently redirect them, reminding them of God's faithfulness. Sing psalms and hymns. Always hold a heart full of thankfulness.

I've found that writing down, photographing, or telling a friend what God has done for me helps strengthen my memory of his goodness. Our joy as believers doesn't rely on being given everything we want but on the assurance of God's nearness and remembering his grace with joy. Recounting the ways God has been good to you in the past can help you meet even the hardest trials with joy.

In Context

I've listed some of my favorite passages on gratitude below. After reading each passage in your Bible, use the space provided to respond to one (or both) of these questions:

> **What does this teach you about how and why to practice gratitude?**
>
> **What does this reveal to you about who God is?**

You can also choose to simply write out the passage. Writing the Word of God helps solidify it in our hearts.

1 Chronicles 16:34

Psalm 107:1

Isaiah 12:4-5

Colossians 2:6-7

A Gentle Invitation into Gratitude

How can reciting what you're grateful for help you better remember who God is?

How would gratitude change your life?

Prayer

Jesus, you made a way for me to have peace. Through your death and resurrection, you brought me into your presence.

Let gratitude for what you have done be the antidote to my anxieties. Remind me of all the things you have done for me to strengthen my faith today.

Give me the chance to share with others the works you have done so I can build my community in faith.

Digging Deeper into Gratitude

If you have bonus time, I invite you to explore an additional verse on gratitude. Write out James 1:17 on an index card or Post-it so you can refer to it throughout your week.

Now let's take some time to look deeply at James 1:17. We want to see this verse in its context, understand the words used, and discover its meaning.

James 1:17 repeats and rephrases key ideas, like "good" and "perfect" or "from above" and "coming down." What do you think James is emphasizing through this repetition?

Every good and perfect gift is from above, coming down from the Father of lights, who does not change like shifting shadows.

JAMES 1:17

What descriptive words and imagery are used to make this verse vivid?

How would you express the idea of this verse in your own words?

A SECOND LOOK AT Gratitude

I wandered through the drizzling rain over the taupe gray hill, pink plastic camera in hand. Ordinary cobwebs were transformed into gauzy lace; the full creek gurgled merrily.

I had been feeling down all week. The gray days had seeped into my mood, casting a dingy hue onto everything that happened to me. Finally, in desperation to feel *something*, I grabbed my canvas coat and my camera and headed out to the hills behind our house. In just about an hour, the fresh air and beauty chased away the blahs and filled my heart with gratitude as I recorded with photographs the beauty of the world I live in. I returned with pink cheeks and a heart pulsing with happiness. That day taught me an important lesson about how to access gratitude when I don't feel it.

Awe, when experienced in nature, is mysteriously good for us in a way that researchers have spent years trying to understand. It eases stress and improves emotional health, and more importantly it connects us to God and a world larger than our personal human experience, opening the door to gratitude for the life and beauty around us.

Sadly, the human memory is more inclined to remember the hard things we experience than the lovely moments. I only remember that beautiful moment I had fifteen years ago because I was in a journaling phase and wrote it down. I've never reread the entry, but writing about my experience cemented it into my memory.

The Bible tells us over 150 times to be grateful.[9] I think this encouragement is given so frequently because when we mark "every good and perfect gift," as James 1:17 says, we are more likely to remember them—and the one who gave them to us.

Scholars generally agree that the book of James was written by Jesus' brother James. After the resurrection, he joined Peter to become a prominent leader of the church in Jerusalem. This is incredible, since Jesus' siblings were initially closed to his message (John 7:5). However, some, like James, were converted after witnessing the resurrection. James was known as a devout follower of Christ. In fact, tradition says that his knees became so calloused from prayer that they looked like a camel's knees. Ultimately, he was martyred for his faith.

Even though the book of James is found toward the end of our Bible, it was likely the first epistle, written as persecution against the church was just beginning. This is why the book begins by encouraging believers to have courage in the face of suffering. Against human instinct, believers are to count it joy when they meet trials. Why? Because a tested faith results in patience and steadiness. The more we depend on God's strength during trials, the more our faith grows and the less power our circumstances have over us.

In James 1:13-15, we're reminded of the character of God. When we are tempted to do evil, it isn't from God. Rather, it is our own fallen desires that tempt us. Similarly, we know that the things we suffer aren't at the hand of God but the result of a world broken by sin, which creates painful circumstances, even for the believer.

Understanding this context allows James 1:17 to shine. In the middle of pain, James declares to the church that good and perfect gifts come from God. Just like my long walk with a plastic camera helped me to see and remember beauty, James is helping the early church reframe their suffering by pointing to God's goodness around them. Even amid all the trials, they can joyfully remember not only the good gifts from God but that he himself was the greatest gift!

Before the creation of the world, God had a plan to reunite us to himself. When Adam and Eve saw the world filled with despair because of their sin, he had already planned the rescue. He painted rescue all over the Old Testament so that his people would never forget his love for them. And when the time was right, he stooped down to earth to enter the womb. He was born, he lived sinlessly, and then he died and rose again.

God is perfect. He is steadfast. When we sin against him or are ungrateful, he doesn't take back his forgiveness; instead, he offers us life. He proved his love by dying for us while we were still sinners (Romans 5:8), and he continues to love us even when we fail. When humankind crucified him, he redeemed us. He endured the cross so that we might have a life to be grateful for.

Because Jesus lived, died, and resurrected, we can face our trials and even grow our faith and express overwhelming gratitude in the middle of those trials. But here is the best part: We don't have to squeeze out gratitude on our own. God himself gently tends us into gratitude. It is an extension of his work and flows from the Holy Spirit living in us.

Practicing gratitude involves a heart change. We must realize that we aren't the source of good in our lives. Good things aren't something we earn, attract, or achieve; we receive all good things from God. When we name the good gifts he is giving, it strengthens our understanding of our own stories in the middle of God's bigger story.

Writing down what God has done in and for you is one way to remember the good and perfect gifts from your heavenly Father. But gratitude can be practiced in other ways too. It can look like celebrating a good day by turning on worship music. It can be going out to dinner with friends to celebrate something good and beginning with a prayer of thankfulness. It could also be having a photo in your home that reminds you of answered prayer, or taping up a verse that has special meaning to you. There are so many beautiful ways to give thanks!

Additional Context

I've listed some more of my favorite passages on gratitude below. After reading each passage in your Bible, use the space provided to respond to one (or both) of these questions:

> **What does this teach you about how and why to practice gratitude?**
>
> **What does this reveal to you about who God is?**

You can also choose to simply write out the passage. Writing the Word of God helps solidify it in our hearts.

Psalm 103:1-4

Psalm 118:24

Hebrews 13:15

2 Corinthians 9:15

A Second Invitation into Gratitude

How might having a posture of gratitude change the way you respond to circumstances in your life?

What is something in your life that might be hard to see with gratitude? Take some time to pray about it and ask God to help you see where gratitude fits in.

Meditation

It's so easy for us to overthink what meditation is, but it's simply the things we think about repeatedly. Spiritual meditation is when we listen to the Word of God, reflect on his works, remember what he has done, and think over his laws, always with a heart change in mind. Meditating may feel mundane, but it changes your life, your attitude, and your thoughts.

Video Notes

DISCUSSION AND REFLECTION QUESTIONS

- What have you been taught about meditation?
- Is there anyone in your life who practices meditation well?
- Who are some people who modeled meditation in the Bible? What happened when they listened for the voice of God? (If you can't think of examples, see 1 Kings 19:9-18; Joshua 1:8; and Genesis 24:63.)

To access the video session, use the instructions in the front of your Bible study book.

A Record of God's Gentle Tending

Sometimes we think God doesn't meet with us, when really we just don't pause long enough to notice what he's already doing. Take a moment to record how God is tending you.

Have you ever repeated a verse from Scripture or song lyrics to help in a difficult moment? How did those truths transform your perspective or replace the lies you believed?

Finding Meditation in the Word

Write out Psalm 19:14 on an index card or Post-it so you can refer to it throughout your week.

Now let's take some time to look deeply at Psalm 19:14. We want to see this verse in its context, understand the words used, and discover its meaning.

What are the key words in this verse?

May the words of my
mouth
and the meditation of
my heart
be acceptable to you,
LORD, my rock and my
Redeemer.

PSALM 19:14

What does this verse ask for that is different from the verse before it (verse 13)?

David, the author of Psalm 19, was a shepherd. Shepherds spent a lot of time alone in fields both day and night. How do you think that experience helped or impacted his thoughts and experience of meditation?

LET'S DIG INTO

Meditation

What we consistently think about changes the way we see our lives. I remember the year we bought our Toyota Sienna. I had never noticed Siennas before, but after we bought ours, I noticed them everywhere.

A less benign example is the negative self-talk that used to constantly run through my head: *You're a horrible friend. Your house is always a mess. That was a stupid thing to say; you always say the wrong thing.* These words I spoke to myself caused me to live in guilt and fear. Living in guilt and fear caused me more anxiety, which only increased the behaviors I was criticizing myself for.

When I started focusing instead on what Jesus had done for me, it changed the way I viewed my life. I began replacing the lies with these truths: *He is transforming me daily to nurture as he nurtures. My home is not a shrine to my good taste but a place of welcome. God's Spirit will guide my words.* I realized I had the freedom to change the words I spoke to myself, and this caused me to be more intentional and wiser as I moved forward.

We can look to the book of Psalms for help in changing our thoughts. It contains poetry written over many years by worship leaders, poets, priests, and kings. These psalms provided a template for prayer and functioned as a songbook of worship. Each psalm had special meaning, and many were intended to be sung during specific times of day, seasons, and festivals. Through singing and reciting, the people of Israel were able to meditate on the Word and law of God, even though they didn't own personal copies of Scripture like we do today.

The Psalms reminded God's people of the powerful works he had done for them over the centuries. As they sang psalms together, they taught the commandments of God to their children and shared stories of his deliverance (Deuteronomy 6:7-8). Animal sacrifices were required by the law as payment for sin, so as they tended their sheep, goats, and pigeons for sacrifice all year, they would have been reminded of their brokenness and the promise of redemption (Leviticus 1-7). God created these routines to help his people fix their eyes on him. But if you know the Old Testament, you know that the Israelites had a habit of forgetting how much God loved them and the work he had promised to do for them.

We also struggle to remember the love God has for us. We believe that what others think of us defines us. So we hurry to clean the house before guests arrive and end up being unkind to those who live with us, convinced that the appearance of our homes reveals something about our worth. We spend hours in front of our closet trying to pick what to wear because we feel that our identity is tied to the way we dress our bodies. We make jokes at the expense of others to be seen as funny even though we know it's unkind. We deprive our bodies of sleep by staying up into the early hours of the morning, studying to get the perfect grades. These things give us a good image but leave us on the treadmill, running hard for more.

Just as he did for the Israelites, God has provided us with rhythms and routines that can reorient our focus. Jesus invited us into a ritual of remembrance the night before he died: "On the night when he was betrayed, the Lord Jesus took bread, and when he had given thanks, broke it, and said, 'This is my body, which is for you. Do this in remembrance of me.' In the same way also he took the cup, after supper, and said, 'This cup is the new covenant in my blood. Do this, as often as you drink it, in remembrance of me'" (1 Corinthians 11:23-25).

Through psalms and sacrifices, the Israelites remembered the promise that a Savior would come, and we celebrate that he did come. He came so that by his wounds, he could heal us from the wicked words that run through our heads. He prepared a new identity for us and gently tends us into a new way of living. As modern Christians, we meditate on Christ when we come to Communion, pray before meals, and attend church. But God knows that even when our intentions are good, we are in the habit of forgetting. We forget that he is kind and that his commands are for our own good and inner peace. That is why we meditate—to refocus our minds and hearts.

The ancient Israelites would have been familiar with the concept of meditation (see Psalm 1:2), but it's something that's become lost, confused, and paganized in our culture. Christian meditation is not an attempt to empty one's mind but rather to fill it with God's voice and his commands.

In Luke 11:24-26, Jesus told a story about a person who was entirely taken over by evil spirits. Supernaturally, these evil spirits were cast out, but since they did not fill their thoughts with anything in place of the evil spirits, the problem just reoccurred, and it was even worse the second time. Detaching ourselves from negativity isn't enough; after redeeming us, God fills us with his Spirit. As we remember and recite his goodness it becomes more tightly knit to our identity.

God can sanctify our bodies, imaginations, and desires. We can view our worries and anxieties through the reality of a Savior who redeems and loves us. Cultivating this continual awareness allows us to open our hands and release those worries to his care.

It's so easy for us to overthink what meditation is, but the reality is that meditation is natural to humans. We meditate when we listen to the Word of God, reflect on his works, remember what he has done, and think over his laws, always with a heart change in mind. Meditating may feel mundane, but it leads to profound life transformation. Theologian Dietrich Bonhoeffer defined personal meditation as taking brief passages of Scripture and reflecting deeply on the words—sometimes for a week at a time.[10] So we are already on the right track with the work we've been doing in this study!

My favorite form of meditation is pausing in my busy day to notice small details that remind me of the kindness of God and his salvation. While drinking my morning cup of coffee, I might glance at the weeds near my back deck and reflect that the weeds in this life are temporary and redeemed in the new creation. Or while chopping fruit to eat, I pause to remember that God promises to grow the fruit of his Spirit in me.

Many of us have quiet, hidden moments built into our days—such as rocking a child or settling into bed just before we fall asleep. This week I encourage you to intentionally take a verse, picture, or phrase with you to that quiet place in your life and use the stillness to remember God's kindness to you.

In Context

I've listed some of my favorite passages on meditation below. After reading each passage in your Bible, use the space provided to respond to one (or both) of these questions:

> **What does this teach you about how and why to practice meditation?**
>
> **What does this reveal to you about who God is?**

You can also choose to simply write out the passage. Writing the Word of God helps solidify it in our hearts.

Psalm 1:2

Joshua 1:8

Psalm 119:15

Isaiah 26:3-4

A Gentle Invitation into Meditation

Psalm 1:2 encourages us to "delight . . . in the LORD's instruction." What are some practical ways to delight in God's instructions to you this week?

Is there a quiet moment already built into your day that you could use to meditate on God's truth? What might that look like?

Prayer

Spirit, thank you for coming and living in us while we wait for Christ to come again. You come to me in moments when I'm self-absorbed and remind me of truths I've forgotten.

Please bring your words to my mind often and teach your truths to my heart. As I remember your truths, bring me your peace.

Digging Deeper into Meditation

If you have bonus time, I invite you to explore an additional verse on meditation. Write out Philippians 4:8 on an index card or Post-it so you can refer to it throughout your week.

Now let's take some time to look deeply at Philippians 4:8. We want to see this verse in its context, understand the words used, and discover its meaning.

List the types of things we should think about according to this verse, then look up the definitions of these words. Does anything surprise you?

Finally brothers and sisters, whatever is true, whatever is honorable, whatever is just, whatever is pure, whatever is lovely, whatever is commendable—if there is any moral excellence and if there is anything praiseworthy—dwell on these things.

PHILIPPIANS 4:8

What do you think it means to "dwell" on something? What might that look like in everyday life?

The apostle Paul is the author of Philippians. What does the next verse (Philippians 4:9) reveal about Paul's ministry?

A SECOND LOOK AT

Meditation

I remember once hearing a story about a rescue cat who had lost all her kittens at birth. She was sad, depressed, and refusing food. In a box next to her was a nest of baby squirrels who were struggling to survive after being blown from a tree. Desperate, the shelter decided to see if the mother cat would adopt the baby squirrels.

Hours later the squirrels were nursing from the mother cat, and she was licking them clean. They curled up next to the beat of her heart to grow and sleep. As time passed, the baby squirrels began to mimic the cat, believing they were kittens. Their identity was shaped by imprinting on a cat.

Our identities are shaped by our environments, the people closest to us, and the labels placed on us from childhood. Perhaps you've heard someone say about you, "Oh, she's the *quiet* one." You could easily replace *quiet* with any number of adjectives like *bossy, anxious, loud, giving, creative,* etc. The more we hear and dwell on these labels, the more we begin to internalize them as part of our identity.

Once our identity has been formed, it can be hard to adjust. Sometimes the influences in our lives can take us far; other times they create negative patterns we have to set aside as we rediscover our true identities.

In today's verse, Paul encourages the Philippian church to look to God's truth to form their identity. From its founding, this church faced many challenges. In Acts 16 we read of a dramatic response to the gospel when Paul and Silas first preached the gospel in Philippi. But before long, their ministry was met with opposition. When the power of God through Paul delivered a girl from the possession of evil, her owners, whose livelihood depended on her demonic fortune-telling abilities, were outraged and had Paul and Silas thrown into prison.

This is where the story starts to shift. After Paul and Silas were thrown into prison, there was an earthquake that opened all the doors of the jail, allowing for a jailbreak. When the jailer saw all the doors open, he knew he would be humiliated and executed for failing his job so thoroughly, so he drew his sword to end his anguish. But Paul called out and explained that all the prisoners were still there. Through the supernatural events of that night, the jailer became a believer. The next morning, the town realized Paul and Silas were Roman citizens, which meant they couldn't be imprisoned there. They were freed and forced to leave the city (Acts 16:25-40).

The new little church, however, could not escape its time and place and continued to face persecution. It would have been easy for them to forget the supernatural parts of their story and assume false labels such as powerless, doomed, or forgotten, causing them to be closed off or guarded toward those outside their faith community.

Knowing the story of the Philippian church allows us to understand why Paul encouraged them to stay focused on beautiful truths. When we try to empty our minds of negativity or summon the energy to think positively and unlock new spiritual levels, eventually we crash out. As humans there is an end to the well of energy we can muster. We can only draw from what we have already stored up. But Paul is not telling them to work harder at positive thinking. Paul is encouraging them to simply focus their attention on the good things God has already provided.

As Christians, the best way we can dwell on what is good and lovely is to remember the work of the one who was fully good on our behalf and laid his perfect life down so that we can have freedom and truth. We don't have to summon the energy to go to a mountaintop or monthlong retreat to think over truths that are honorable, just, and lovely. Jesus came down to be God with us, and he sent his Spirit to live inside us. He resisted temptation (Matthew 4:1-11) and fulfilled the law on our behalf.

In the middle of hard times, as we internally recite what God has done, our secure attachment to God is strengthened. We know that babies who don't have face-to-face time with their mothers often end up with attachment disorders. This not only prevents them from thriving but also causes them to be more distrustful of others for the rest of their lives. God's face is always toward you. Turning your thoughts and gaze to him in small moments throughout your day cultivates peace, trust, and a calm reliance on him.

This form of meditation transforms not just our souls but our way of living as well. As we call into remembrance his work in us, the fruit of the Spirit flows more freely from us. Our lives are marked by qualities like love, joy, peace, and patience (Galatians 5:22-23). From time spent meditating on the law of God, we are given wisdom to know how it applies to our lives and interpersonal situations.

Paul wasn't calling the Philippian church to a new way of life but rather reminding them of the ways that God's people had always remembered his work. All through the Old Testament we see believers being called to listen to the reading of God's Word, remember his works, and repeat truths about his law, character, and promises. Meditating on truth changed the Philippian church. Rather than drifting into despondency over their hard path, they became known as a church that was incredibly generous and mostly lived at peace with one another even in the face of external pressure.

So as you make your coffee, lay down to sleep, sit at the bedside of a loved one, or chauffeur others from place to place, remember the work of God in you. Listen to the true Word of God read aloud, remember the honorable work he has done in your life, and repeat to yourself truths about God's just character and promises to you. Allow your identity to be formed by his character.

Dwelling in this kind of meditation rarely stays internal. From it bursts joy, changed behavior, repentance, and obedience. It leads us to the realization that God is good and wants to tend us gently into truth. We can give up guilt when we fall back into negative thought patterns and recenter on his kindness and faithfulness. It will get easier over time as we discover that we always find joy and peace in his presence.

Additional Context

I've listed some more of my favorite passages on meditation below. After reading each passage in your Bible, use the space provided to respond to one (or both) of these questions:

What does this teach you about how and why to practice meditation?

What does this reveal to you about who God is?

You can also choose to simply write out the passage. Writing the Word of God helps solidify it in our hearts.

Psalm 4:8

Psalm 63:6

Psalm 143:6

Philippians 4:8

A Second Invitation into Meditation

Who do you want to become? What is a truth you can think about for the next hour, day, or week to help you toward that?

What does a biblical understanding of meditation show you about God and the way he desires to meet with you each day?

Gently Tending

Your Daily Walk

Spiritual transformation may begin in the quiet moments of each day as God tends your heart and mind. But as you spend more time with your Savior, the way you live out your faith will be transformed as well. You aren't created to be alone reading your Bible and praying all day but rather to fulfill Matthew 5:16 and "let your light shine before others" so they might be led to praise God. As you incorporate the following disciplines into your daily rhythms, invite God to gently tend to all you think, say, and do so you can bring glory to him in your daily walk.

Humility

Humility is a means to freedom from self-centeredness. When we imitate the humility of Christ, we are freed from self-pity, groveling, bitterness, and performance. When Jesus served, it didn't make him less than God. If we seek to be first we will lose our grasp on what it means to follow Jesus, but the more we release our entitlement, the closer we find ourselves to the heart of the gospel.

Video Notes

DISCUSSION AND REFLECTION QUESTIONS

- Is there someone in your life whom you admire for their humility?
- What are some ways a person might demonstrate unhealthy behavior as they try to practice humility?
- Reflect on a few of the highs and lows you've experienced in your life. What has each moment revealed to you about humility or your dependence on God?

To access the video session, use the instructions in the front of your Bible study book.

A Record of God's Gentle Tending

Sometimes we think God doesn't meet with us, when really we just don't pause long enough to notice what he's already doing. Take a moment to record how God is tending you.

Reflect on a time when you were asked to do something hard that required sacrifice. How did God sustain you as you set yourself aside?

Finding Humility in the Word

Write out Ephesians 5:18, 21 on an index card or Post-it so you can refer to it throughout your week.

> Now let's take some time to look deeply at Ephesians 5:18, 21. We want to see this passage in its context, understand the words used, and discover its meaning.

What would you say is the key word in this passage? Why?

Be filled by the Spirit . . . submitting to one another in the fear of Christ.

EPHESIANS 5:18, 21

What do you think "the fear of Christ" refers to? Look up Ephesians 5:18, 21 in several translations to see if the concept becomes clearer.

Can you think of anyone in the Old Testament who demonstrated the practice of "submitting to one another," humbly setting aside their own desires for the good of another? (If you can't think of an example, see Ruth 1:6-18.)

LET'S DIG INTO

Humility

I recently came across a short audio clip on social media that says, "You say you would die for your kids, but would you live for them?" Usually this audio is accompanied by videos of parents working out to improve their health. While the clip focuses on improving physical health and wellness, in the context of biblical humility, I think it touches on something profound. Many of us declare to our loved ones, "I would die for you," and yet often we won't do the hard things that would benefit them, or we give in when what they want inconveniences us. We sometimes value our happiness and comfort more than the good of our children.

I've encountered this struggle many times as a parent. When one of our children was only a year old, every morning, as soon as his eyes popped open, he wanted to be fed more than just a bowl of cereal. This small human ate five eggs for breakfast each day. His appetite reminded me of Gaston's song from *Beauty and the Beast,* where he boasts of eating "four dozen eggs" each day as a lad.[11]

Dragging myself out of bed every morning to make breakfast when my stomach wouldn't be ready to eat for another hour felt hard. But if you've ever been in a caregiving role for children, you know it's the least wild thing motherhood demands.

It feels funny to say this about something so ordinary, but in technical Bible terms I was "submitting" myself to the needs of my child. I was humbling myself to serve him, doing what was in his best interest even though it wasn't what I wanted to do.

There are many things in the Bible that seem illogical by human standards. For instance, "Whoever wants to save his life will lose it, but whoever loses his life because of me will find it" (Matthew 16:25) and "When I am weak, then I am strong" (2 Corinthians 12:10).

Deciding "who is in charge" is another one of these paradoxes that even seasoned believers get upside down. Jesus tells us, "Whoever wants to become great among you must be your servant" (Matthew 20:26) and "Many who are first will be last, and the last first" (Matthew 19:30). This is the opposite of how the world understands power and greatness.

During his ministry on earth, Jesus willingly gave his time, energy, rest, and even his life for our benefit. He reminded us that putting others first is how we best live according to his Kingdom, and he instructed us to follow his example of humility.

When we look at the life of Jesus, we see him demonstrate humility—and the closely related practice of submission—in every circumstance. Yet many church sermons on this discipline tend to focus on "submission" only in the context of marriage. We must not forget that submission isn't about being in charge, and as believers, we are called to submit in *all* our relationships from a place of love. As mothers we submit to the cries of our nursing babies. In friendship we allow the other person to choose where we'll meet up for lunch. At work we see our coworkers as souls to be loved rather than obstacles to our advancement up the career ladder.

Without the reality of the cross, fighting for what we need would be necessary to get ahead. Everything we see is all that there would ever be. If we wanted life to have any meaning, we would have to take it for ourselves. Stepping on others to get the best in our career would be a matter of course. Strong-arming our friends to get what we want would be necessary—after all, we only live once.

But when Jesus died and resurrected, he conquered death. We don't have to fight to get what's best on this earth anymore. When Jesus rose from the grave, he opened eternity up to us so that at the end of our lives on earth we can walk through the gates of heaven to live forever with him. Knowing that this world isn't all there is frees us to give freely to others and serve the way Jesus served. As the old hymn says, "This world is not my home, I'm just a-passing through."[12]

Healthy relationships grow among believers as we give others our best and the same love is given in return. In this way, we demonstrate the selfless love of God. Humbling ourselves to the needs of others becomes a joy. We are wholeheartedly dedicated to the good of others.

Humility, when practiced correctly, enables us to shine God's love in our daily lives. But we also must acknowledge that teachings on humility and submission have been abused. Sin took something beautiful and manipulated it into something dark. Power-hungry leaders have used it as a tool of domination to control instead of carefully applying Christ's teachings to their own lives.

Becoming submissive isn't the goal of submission; rather submission is a means to freedom from self-centeredness. As we imitate the humility of Christ, we're set free from self-pity, groveling, bitterness, and performance. When Jesus served, it didn't make him less than God. If we seek our advancement in the Kingdom, we'll lose the true meaning of following Christ. But letting go of our entitlement brings us closer to the heart of the gospel (Matthew 10:39).

When we give up our demand to "get our due" and to take "an eye for an eye" (Exodus 21:24), we can freely follow Jesus, who laid down his life by his own choice (John 10:18). We will begin to truly love our enemies (Matthew 5:44). Only then will we discover that our happiness doesn't depend on getting what we want.

This isn't to abolish all authority but to upend a "pecking order." Authority is a way to preserve the safety of the community, not a means to manipulate for personal gain. A good leader will miss out on benefits and place themselves in the crossfire in order to prioritize the needs of those they're called to serve.

This is the context we easily miss when reading passages on submission. When Paul gave these instructions to the early church, wives and slaves were legally bound by Roman law to obey those in authority over them. Allowing them to render their service as a gift to God gave them agency where legally they had none. And what's truly revolutionary about these passages is that they applied the Christian ethic of submission to masters and husbands too. Those in authority were now biblically required to submit to the needs of those under them by loving and caring for them more than even their own bodies.

This means that all the ways you humble yourself to the needs of others, both easy and hard, can be given to God. You don't have to fight to maintain your own interests; instead, you can invest in the interests of others (Philippians 2:4) because you live considering eternity. This week, as you prepare a meal, nurse your baby, or care for an aging spouse, remember that no act is "too small" to be given as a gift to God.

In Context

I've listed some of my favorite passages on humility below. After reading each passage in your Bible, use the space provided to respond to one (or both) of these questions:

What does this teach you about how and why to practice humility?

What does this reveal to you about who God is?

You can also choose to simply write out the passage. Writing the Word of God helps solidify it in our hearts.

Matthew 23:12

Philippians 2:3-4

James 4:10

Proverbs 11:2

A Gentle Invitation into Humility

What does the biblical understanding of humility show you about God's character?

As you reflect on the practice of humility, how do you feel God gently tending your heart toward change?

Prayer

Jesus, you humbled yourself to death on the cross! It's hard to comprehend that the King of the universe willingly came to earth as a baby, entirely dependent on the care of others and not even able to feed himself. You shared in our weakness and embraced a humility that led to physical death.

When I am tempted to control and manipulate others to do what is best for me, pause me. Transform my heart to find joy in placing others ahead of myself. Make my heart more like yours.

Digging Deeper into Humility

If you have bonus time, I invite you to explore an additional passage on humility. Write out Philippians 2:3-4 on an index card or Post-it so you can refer to it throughout your week.

Now let's take some time to look deeply at Philippians 2:3-4. We want to see this passage in its context, understand the words used, and discover its meaning.

What are the two contrasting ways of life shown in this passage?

Do nothing out of selfish ambition or conceit, but in humility consider others as more important than yourselves. Everyone should look not to his own interests, but rather to the interests of others.

PHILIPPIANS 2:3-4

What repeated words do you see? Why do you think these are important?

How would you express the idea of this passage in your own words?

A SECOND LOOK AT

Humility

As evening approached, I perched on the edge of a recliner in a nursing home, watching Shirley Temple with a client in her nineties. We had been that way for nearly an hour—talking, laughing, and singing along with the TV. Moments later, I was holding her hand while she paced the floor as sundowning syndrome set in. It was like a switch flipped and she was grasping for memories that were no longer there. Eyes that had been closed in peace were now flashing with anger as she shouted at me words I didn't understand. Then she came at me to fight. Shocked, I stepped back as she quickly closed the gap between us and grabbed my wrists.

These moments working in home health came with opportunities to choose between "eye for an eye" living and turning the other cheek (Exodus 21:24; Matthew 5:39). I took a deep breath and started singing, "You are my sunshine, my only sunshine."[13] Her face softened and tears caught in her eyelashes. As she joined me with a quavering voice in the old familiar song, her shoulders relaxed. I successfully changed her into pajamas and settled her into bed, gently whispering the end to the song.

As she drifted off to sleep, I settled myself back into the recliner to wait for the end of my shift. Surprisingly, at the end of every evening, there was a sense of overwhelming gratification in having given up my evening to create even just one night of peace for another human.

Today's passage, Philippians 2:3-4, encourages us to live according to our identity in Christ and follow his example. It precedes a passage of Philippians known as "the Christ Hymn,"[14] which celebrates Jesus' willingness to become human, suffer, and die for our salvation. Even though he was fully God, he didn't parade around demanding special treatment but rather became a servant to all.

Each sin we are warned against in the Bible has a corresponding freedom, and this holds true for the warning against "selfish ambition." We aren't asked to move into humility so we can be a doormat or enslaved to others but so we can find freedom.[15] To gain the freedom that submission brings, we must lay down our own wishes and ask God to soften the hard shell of stubbornness.

This requires a genuine release of control. Sometimes, when we're asked for our input on something, we say, "I don't care"—though deep down we *do* care. Then, when the other person doesn't guess properly what we wanted, we nurse our hurt feelings. This type of false humility can be dangerous and does not bring us the freedom Christ offers.

Humility is difficult because humans are all born self-obsessed. While the instinct to care for our bodies is good, sin has twisted our desires so that we often become fixated on self-preservation at all costs. We become angry or discontented when we don't get what we want or when someone ignores our wishes (whether those wishes are stated or implied). If left unchecked, this anger can fester into bitterness that we carry for a lifetime. For others of us, our self-centeredness may show up as extreme anxiety, as we try to plan and control every detail of our lives to achieve the outcome we want.

Both ways of moving through life put us at the center of the narrative. But biblical humility calls us to put Christ as the center of the story. The goal is not to verbally abuse yourself but to experience the complete "freedom of self-forgetfulness," as Tim Keller put it.[16] It's not thinking less of yourself but thinking of yourself less.[17]

If you're like me, that may feel impossible at times. Be encouraged: After Jesus conquered death and rose again, he said that he was returning to heaven for our benefit, so he could send the Holy Spirit to comfort and guide us. We don't have to claw our way out of self-centeredness alone. As we remember the work Christ accomplished and live the way he lived, we will start to bear fruit and look more like him. This fruit isn't called "the fruit of the Christian" or "the fruit of the do-gooder." It's the fruit of the *Spirit*. It's the way we start to look like Jesus as we depend on him to guide our actions.

Because of Christ's work in our lives, we can have a humble spirit of grace that sees the needs of others. We can give this grace without anger and bitterness only when we realize the grace that has been extended to us—when we know that we are truly seen, known, and loved by God. Then we can give up feelings of entitlement and seek the good of others.

This brings us to the most radical part of Jesus' teachings. He said, "If anyone wants to follow after me, let him deny himself, take up his cross, and follow me" (Mark 8:34). Following Christ means walking in step with the one who "humbled himself by becoming obedient to the point of death—even death on a cross" (Philippians 2:8). The cross provides an example of doing what is difficult on behalf of another. Jesus did the ultimate difficult thing on our behalf so we can do hard things too.

Though it's humanly impossible to live the perfect life Jesus lived, through the power of his Spirit we can choose humility over selfishness when we do things like opening our hearts to love a difficult neighbor. We can rejoice with a mom who is announcing her pregnancy when we wish we were pregnant too. When a friend faces the consequences of their bad choices, we can resist the urge to say, "I told you so," and instead meet them with compassion and empathy (Romans 12:15). We can listen to a family member tell their story of pain again without demanding that they "just get over it." We may need to choose to have a hard conversation when we would rather stay quiet. Or perhaps humility looks like setting a boundary with someone who is sliding into toxic behaviors without using words of derision or anger. We can take an evening to serve the homeless a dinner or offer a morning to care for a toddler.

If we do all these things and don't receive the thanks we feel we deserve for our kindness, wisdom, and time, we don't have to be angry. We weren't humbling ourselves for their thanks or praise. We submit to others and love because he first loved us. The way Christ came and lived and called us to live is almost always upside down from what's expected in this world. I promise that as you practice giving up yourself, you will find joy.

Additional Context

I've listed some more of my favorite passages on humility below. After reading each passage in your Bible, use the space provided to respond to one (or both) of these questions:

What does this teach you about how and why to practice humility?

What does this reveal to you about who God is?

You can also choose to simply write out the passage. Writing the Word of God helps solidify it in our hearts.

2 Chronicles 7:14

Micah 6:8

1 Peter 5:6

Ephesians 4:2

A Second Invitation into Humility

Sometimes embracing new spiritual practices can feel hard. What, if anything, about humility makes you uncomfortable? Take a moment to pray over your concerns, remembering that Jesus meets each one with gentleness and compassion.

Which fruits of the Spirit do you think are necessary to grow in humility (see Galatians 5:22-23)? Choose one and reflect on how you can intentionally invite God to cultivate that virtue in you this week.

Service

Service may seem like bondage to another, but in reality, it's freedom through Christ's death and resurrection from the rat race of self-promotion. Knowing that Jesus calls us to serve keeps us from grasping for positions of importance. Our willingness to give of ourselves, our time, and our money to care for others is the way we answer the call of the New Testament to not return to the bondage we were rescued from. You're free; now live *free*![18]

Video Notes

DISCUSSION AND REFLECTION QUESTIONS

- Have you ever felt that your willingness to serve was taken advantage of? How did you handle that situation?
- What is one way you love to serve? What kind of service is hard for you?
- Rank the jobs in your church from most appreciated to least appreciated. How can you encourage someone who is serving in an underappreciated role?

To access the video session, use the instructions in the front of your Bible study book.

A Record of God's Gentle Tending

Sometimes we think God doesn't meet with us, when really we just don't pause long enough to notice what he's already doing. Take a moment to record how God is tending you.

Have you seen an example of someone serving God well? How did that impact your life?

Finding Service in the Word

Write out Galatians 5:13 on an index card or Post-it so you can refer to it throughout your week.

Now let's take some time to look deeply at Galatians 5:13. We want to see this verse in its context, understand the words used, and discover its meaning.

This verse encourages service and discourages living to satisfy "the flesh." How would you describe the difference between these two ways of living?

You were called to be free, brothers and sisters; only don't use this freedom as an opportunity for the flesh, but serve one another through love.

GALATIANS 5:13

If a child or unbeliever read this verse, what questions might they have?

Freedom is emphasized in this verse. Make your best guess at what the Galatian Christians were set free from. (If you're stuck, read Galatians 5:1-15 for hints.)

LET'S DIG INTO

Service

I was tempted to feel like all the work had been a waste. The amount of money I was being paid for this job meant I was basically volunteering.

My husband gently asked me, "Did you do it to get rich?" I smiled at him. He knew exactly what question to ask. He was right. I had chosen to do this project because I love kids and wanted them to know and love Jesus.

I was reminded that because I serve Jesus, my time and effort can't be stolen. Every hour is already his. He uses my life in domestic tasks, volunteer projects, and writing. They all bring him glory and bring me joy.

My life cannot be stolen because it is already bought and paid for, and God does beautiful things with everything he is given.

In Galatians 5:13, Paul offers a similar encouragement to the Galatians, who were struggling to remember that Christ's work on the cross had set them free. Some were still imposing old Jewish laws on new believers. Even if they didn't think the law saved new Christians, they believed that it made them better Christians.

We all have ideas about what makes people better humans. As Christians, we may be tempted to think that the "best" and "strongest" believers are those who go to church every Sunday, read through the Scripture in a year, have tons of markings in their Bibles, have "good" testimonies, or know the right things to say when praying.

Even the disciples argued about which of them was the greatest (Luke 22:24). But when we are worried about what others think of us and who is the most respected, we lose sight of the one we are imitating.

At the last supper, Jesus took a towel and washed his disciples' feet. In doing so, he was humiliating himself in front of everyone. The disciples were offended. Culturally, they would have known this meant that they, too, were called to take the humblest positions.[19] In their culture, to wash feet was to take on the contemptuous gaze of others. The modern equivalent would be scrubbing out someone's toilet after they've had the flu or volunteering to clean the snacks and gunk out of the crevices of someone else's car.

After Jesus had finished washing the disciples' feet, he told them to follow his example: "If I, your Lord and Teacher, have washed your feet, you also ought to wash one another's feet" (John 13:14). This must have been a difficult teaching for the disciples to accept. But Jesus showed that the "greatest" Christians are the ones who recognize their need for him, allow him to work in their lives, and follow his example by humbly serving others.

Service seems like bondage to another, but in reality, it's freedom from the rat race of self-promotion and living "for the flesh," as Galatians 5:13 says. When we know that we are called to serve, we can stop grasping for positions of importance.

As humans, it's easy to become overly concerned with our social status. We're constantly assessing where we line up in our friend groups. *Do we have someone who wants to talk to us after church? Are we invited to the "inner circle" dinner on a random Tuesday? Does someone want us to go on a girls' trip with them?*

This struggle with self-centeredness is nothing new. Sin first entered the world when Adam and Eve began thinking that God was holding back something good from them (Genesis 3:6). Eve saw the fruit tree that God had forbidden and thought it would make her life better. So she took and ate. After one bite she realized that what had looked like a good thing was poison that led to death.

Ever since, it has been human nature to grasp for what looks like the best, only for it to turn to sawdust in our hands. You may have experienced broken relationships with brothers or sisters over an inheritance because everyone wants to take the best for themselves. Perhaps your marriage has become a battleground because neither you nor your partner want to give in to what the other wants. Taking the best for yourself seems like it will make you happy, but instead it leaves behind grief and brokenness. We are trapped by our own greed.

Enter Jesus. He left the best of heaven's glory to enter a uterus with not even enough room to stretch out. He was born to a family in poverty. In adulthood, he collected a motley band of followers from drastically different political and educational standings, none in positions of power. Jesus spent his ministry pulled on all sides by people who needed healing, were in distress, or were social outcasts.

He faithfully met those needs but was still so unpopular that the religious leaders had him arrested and killed. He died on a cross—the type of execution reserved for the lowliest criminals in the Roman Empire—to free us from the death tangle of our own grasping. He didn't free us so we can continue to collect the best of everything for ourselves but so we can leave behind the system that defines our value by what we possess.

You have been rescued from bondage and set free. You can live in that freedom!

The service Jesus calls us to is secret (Matthew 6:3-4). It doesn't call attention to how we line up with others. It's service that does not need to be celebrated or appreciated because we are working for God, not angling to become the most successful or the most loved by the people around us. In Jesus' upside-down Kingdom, we aren't picking and choosing who and how we serve or waiting to "feel led," but rather seeing and meeting needs. You know that you are serving well when his Kingdom is expanding and being built.

Often we object to serving and giving up what we want, thinking others will take advantage of us. Richard Foster, a scholar on the spiritual disciplines, says, "Right here we must see the difference between choosing to serve and choosing to be a servant. When we choose to serve, we are still in charge. We decide whom we will serve and when we will serve. . . . But when we choose to be a servant, we give up the right to be in charge."[20] In other words, if we are picking to do what we want rather than doing what Jesus is calling us to do, then we are merely serving, not being a servant of God.

We are called to imitate Christ in service. Today, whether you are listening to a friend, inviting someone over, changing light bulbs, filling out paperwork, or continually regulating your child, you can humbly and freely offer these simple daily tasks to God, seeking to bless and serve others in all you do. He sees what you do in secret. In the process of doing these small acts, you are being transformed to be more like him.

In Context

I've listed some of my favorite passages on service below. After reading each passage in your Bible, use the space provided to respond to one (or both) of these questions:

What does this teach you about how and why to serve?

What does this reveal to you about who God is?

You can also choose to simply write out the passage. Writing the Word of God helps solidify it in our hearts.

Matthew 5:16

Acts 20:35

Romans 12:1

1 Peter 4:10-11

A Gentle Invitation into Service

Sometimes embracing new spiritual practices can feel hard. What, if anything, about serving others makes you uncomfortable? Take a moment to pray over your concerns, remembering that Jesus meets each one with gentleness and compassion.

What are ways you know you're called to serve today?

Prayer

God, you have set before us an example of service. You created the world and everything in it. You rescued your people over and over again and came to earth to serve rather than be served.

Let me follow your example and serve others with gladness. Help me to use my freedom not to indulge myself, but to love freely. Change my heart to be more like yours every single day.

Digging Deeper into Service

If you have bonus time, I invite you to explore an additional passage on service. Write out Philippians 2:4-8 on an index card or Post-it so you can refer to it throughout your week.

Now let's take some time to look deeply at Philippians 2:4-8. We want to see this passage in its context, understand the words used, and discover its meaning.

What words are repeated in this passage? Why do you think they are important?

Everyone should look not to his own interests, but rather to the interests of others.

Adopt the same attitude as that of Christ Jesus,

who, existing in the form of God,
did not consider equality with God
as something to be exploited.
Instead he emptied himself
by assuming the form of a servant,
taking on the likeness of humanity.
And when he had come as a man,
he humbled himself by becoming obedient
to the point of death—
even to death on a cross.

PHILIPPIANS 2:4-8

Who are the key figures mentioned in this passage, and what roles do they play?

Can you describe the two attitudes or heart postures that are contrasted in this passage?

A SECOND LOOK AT

Service

There was a knock at the door. When I opened it, a stranger informed me that my new neighbor's sewer pipes had collapsed, and the neighbor's plumber was going to have to dig into my yard because the city's line was on our side of the fence.

I walked back into the house stunned. I know it seems small, but my kids had spent hours digging and planting our field of sunflowers right by that fence. The tiny shoots had just started to emerge. We also had two mature roses, and our raised garden would have to be moved for the digging.

Our little haven was going to be completely decimated by a mini excavator and a trench. I spent the first day angry. That night I lay awake, anxious about the extra work. Finally, I reached out to friends for prayer.

Not long after, Philippians 2:4 came to mind: "Everyone should look not to his own interests, but rather to the interests of others." I prayed, *Lord, I don't know this neighbor, but help me to consider her needs as more important than my garden.*

He answered. I was blown away later that day when the digging started and I felt perfect peace. My neighbor needed my kindness, and this act was a way to serve her the same way Christ served me.

In today's passage, Philippians 2:4-8, Paul describes how Jesus came to earth to humbly serve and turned power structures upside down. When Jesus declared that "many who are first will be last, and the last first" (Matthew 19:30), he wasn't reversing the pecking order like we tend to believe. Instead, he was dissolving the ranking of humans entirely.[21]

Pecking order is often used to describe the way people sort themselves by rank or status, and that term is so appropriate. We have a flock of beautiful white chickens, and every summer when the Oklahoma heat gets overwhelming the chickens get stressed and take it out on the weakest in the coop. One or two get picked at until their coats are motley. It brings to mind Galatians 5:15: "If you bite and devour one another, watch out, or you will be consumed by one another."

Even as believers in the church, we are tempted to take our stress out on one another. Contrary to the apostle Paul's instructions in Philippians 2:4, we "look to our own interests," trying to prove our status, relieve our internal pressure, or buy social capital.

A more subtle way we might put ourselves first is by serving others for the purpose of making ourselves feel good. Examples of this might include giving gifts to a little child to be the "favorite aunt," hosting the baby shower so we can show off our home, or giving a nice gift at a friend's birthday so they feel obligated to give us a gift as well.

When Christ came to die for us, we had nothing to offer him in return. From the beginning, God had attempted to preserve his people from pain by telling Adam and Eve not to eat of the tree of the knowledge of good and evil, and yet humans flew in the face of his direction. We like to imagine that in the story of salvation, we reach out to grasp the hand of our Savior. But more often we are like that drowning victim they warned you about in swim class—the one who struggles, thrashes, and flails while being saved. We are saved despite our performance, not because of it.

But even though we were at our worst, Christ willingly came, and he served us. Every action was done to glorify God. Because of his love and rescue, we can do the same. But he didn't leave us do this alone. He puts his Holy Spirit in us so that if we are "in step with the Spirit" (Galatians 5:25), love and service for one another will automatically flow out of us.

Spirit-led service frees us from the need to count the cost. We can serve enemies and friends in the exact same way. We can see and serve people in positions of power as well as people who have been abused by power (James 2:1-13).

When we serve with the heart of Christ, we aren't driven by our mood. We serve because we are called to by Christ, not because we feel like it. Many times, if we wait for the feeling of service to strike us, we will miss opportunities to reveal the love of Christ to others. This also means we miss out on an opportunity to love him and feel his love more deeply.

So how can you practice service? I encourage you to start by noticing the little moments each day when you can serve. I think we often despise small acts of service because we can't see the ripple impact they have. But small acts done in love have far-reaching impact.

Maybe for you service means inviting someone over—even when your home isn't perfectly clean—to be present with them.

It could mean listening to another person talk for a long time without interrupting, caring more about hearing their thoughts than sharing your own words.

It might look like giving up what you want and allowing the other person to have the upper hand. Or if you're hanging out with a friend who doesn't often express what she wants, listen to context clues for what she might really like and surprise her.

And if you're doing this study in a group and immediately thought, *Oh, I wonder if someone will do this for me,* set that expectation aside and bring your mind back to Jesus and his service. Allow his Spirit to gently tend your heart close to his, and ask him to reveal to you what he is leading you to do next.

Additional Context

I've listed some more of my favorite passages on service below. After reading each passage in your Bible, use the space provided to respond to one (or both) of these questions:

What does this teach you about how and why to serve?

What does this reveal to you about who God is?

You can also choose to simply write out the passage. Writing the Word of God helps solidify it in our hearts.

Matthew 25:35-40

Ephesians 6:7-8

Hebrews 6:10

1 Peter 1:12

A Second Invitation into Service

What personal goals would you have to lay aside to serve someone else?

How does knowing that Jesus was the ultimate servant change the way you feel about serving others?

Silence

The goal of Christian silence is to remove as many distractions as possible to listen to God through attentiveness and surrender. We don't just read his Word, but we also examine our hearts and apply his truth to our daily lives. This enables us to not only know God's Word but also be gradually transformed by it. God has made it clear repeatedly through Scripture that he wants a relationship with us. He created us to be in communion with him, and silence makes space for that.

Video Notes

DISCUSSION AND REFLECTION QUESTIONS

- What is the longest amount of time you think you could be alone in a cabin?
- Would you describe your current season of life as too loud, too quiet, or somewhere in between?
- What do you find distracts you most often?

To access the video session, use the instructions in the front of your Bible study book.

A Record of God's Gentle Tending

Sometimes we think God doesn't meet with us, when really we just don't pause long enough to notice what he's already doing. Take a moment to record how God is tending you.

Record a beautiful, quiet moment God recently gave you. What did you notice in that silence?

Finding Silence in the Word

Write out Psalm 1:1-2 on an index card or Post-it so you can refer to it throughout your week.

Now let's take some time to look deeply at Psalm 1:1-2. We want to see this passage in its context, understand the words used, and discover its meaning.

According to this passage, what does the righteous person *move away from,* and what do they *move toward*? Put each step of this progression on a different line.

How happy is the one who does not
walk in the advice of the wicked
or stand in the pathway with sinners
or sit in the company of mockers!
Instead, his delight is in the LORD's
instruction,
and he meditates on it day and night.

PSALM 1:1-2

During his life on earth, how did Jesus perfectly demonstrate the righteous living outlined in this passage?

According to this passage, what would the opposite of righteous living look like?

LET'S DIG INTO

Silence

With three young boys, my life is loud, and it's been loud for a long time. So when I heard that a friend was going on a silent retreat—I'm not going to lie—I burned with envy. My friend started explaining to me how our world is full of distractions: Screens ping and demand our attention, schedules are packed, and algorithms are perfectly trained to keep the dopamine hits coming as we swipe from one short video to the next. She said she wanted to practice the discipline of silence by unplugging for a weekend and returning to natural rhythms. Later, as I told my husband about our conversation, I let out a little laugh-sob. "I want to shut it all down too, but that's not possible in my current season."

The next day I woke up to a loud crash and what sounded like two raccoons fighting in a chimney. Heart racing, I dashed out to the living room, only to discover two small boys raging over who got which LEGO head. Wearily, I negotiated peace and made my way over to the coffee maker, thinking about my friend on a silent retreat, before flicking on my screen and swiping. Soon I was laughing at a short video—until another fight broke out. Frustrated, I rushed over to solve the newest problem.

All day I swung between entertainment and frustration. I really wanted to feel the peace of God in my life, but nothing about my current season seemed peace-filled at all. As I thought through the events of the morning, it struck me: What if while I made my coffee I committed to setting my phone down, creating a small space in my day completely free of distraction?

The next morning, I startled awake to a face breathing in my face and a voice whispering, "Is it time to get up?" Slowly,

I placed my feet on the carpeted floor, occupied the little one with something to do, and headed to the coffee maker. I paused as I hit the "on" button, then walked over and placed my phone on the window ledge before starting my coffee ritual.

Sunlight filtered through the steam as the hot espresso streamed into the mug. In the other room I heard laughter as my second child joined the first on the couch. I breathed in and noticed the amazing smells and the feeling of my feet on the vinyl floor. Slowly, the knot in my shoulders relaxed and I felt a bit more rested and ready to greet the day.

It's easy to think that we live in a time and place that is uniquely loud, demanding, and distracting. We can play music at the touch of a screen, listen to podcasts informing us on every topic imaginable, and receive phone calls and voice memos all day long. The pings and dings of devices fracture our attention. All these things come at us, making it hard to focus and settle into silence. With this constant noise comes a rise in anxiety and depression as we rewire our brains for continual dopamine hits.

Even though it seems like today's culture presents us with more distractions than ever before, the battle for quiet and presence is nothing new. In biblical times we see this struggle particularly for women. Customarily women moved into the household of their husband. He would build a room onto his parents' house, and his new wife was added into the hustle and bustle of the already established household, which likely also included his siblings, nieces, and nephews. There was no room for quiet.

Women were also responsible for all the household tasks, allowing little time for silence. In Luke 10:38-42 we see an example of this busyness that probably feels relatable to our current lives. Two sisters, Mary and Martha, were attempting to show their love for Jesus. Martha was busy preparing a big dinner for Jesus and his disciples while Mary sat at Jesus' feet, listening to him teach. After a while, Martha became indignant that her sister wasn't helping with all the work. I don't know about you, but I relate so much to Martha. She was working hard at a job that was good. She was frustrated by seeing her sister sitting with Jesus, seemingly doing nothing. But when Martha asked Jesus to make Mary help her, Jesus said that only "one thing [was] necessary" (Luke 10:42), and Mary had chosen it. Sitting quietly at the feet of Jesus and listening to him was what was necessary.

Silence isn't just removing yourself from the busyness; it is also listening for the voice of God. The Bible is the story of God coming down to talk to his people. God walked and talked with Adam and Eve in the cool of the evening while they lived in Eden. We find that even after the fall when God removed them from the garden for their rebellion against him, he continued to pursue his people, appearing to them in lonely quiet places to talk.

God sent his angel to speak with Hagar, Sarah's handmaid, when she fled to the wilderness to escape an abusive situation (Genesis 16:7), and he answered Rebekah when she inquired why her babies struggled against each other in her womb (Genesis 25:23). God also sent his angel Gabriel to speak with Mary, the mother of Jesus, in the middle of an ordinary day (Luke 1:28). It is a kindness of God that he shows up where his people are.

Ultimately Jesus came down, unprompted, to pay for your life and salvation. His grace entered the world before you were even born, and then his Spirit entered your heart to draw you to himself. Jesus endured the dark, lonely silence from God on the cross so that you might be invited into peaceful eternal communion with him.

The goal of Christian silence is not to avoid all conversation but rather to create space to listen for the voice of God. As we eliminate distractions and focus on God's Word, we can more clearly hear his voice. Then, as we apply that truth to our daily lives (James 1:22), it gradually transforms us. God has made it clear that he wants a relationship with us. He created us to be in communion with him.

Oftentimes we take that to mean we need to read the Bible in a year, join Bible studies, or participate in prayer groups. These are all good things, but when we're already overstimulated and burned out, that feels inaccessible. So we just resign ourselves to the fact that we will never be as close to Jesus as [fill in the blank with your own spiritual role model].

But God is ready to meet you where you are, with what you have in your hands. You don't have to design a day for spiritual silence. Instead, you can claim the quiet moments you already have while putting away the dishes, sitting in traffic, walking for exercise, or sipping your coffee. Use that space to remember his closeness to you and listen for his voice.

In Context

I've listed some of my favorite passages on silence below. After reading each passage in your Bible, use the space provided to respond to one (or both) of these questions:

What does this teach you about how and why to practice silence?

What does this reveal to you about who God is?

You can also choose to simply write out the passage. Writing the Word of God helps solidify it in our hearts.

Psalm 46:10

Psalm 62:5

Habakkuk 2:20

1 Kings 19:12

A Gentle Invitation into Silence

Sometimes embracing new spiritual practices can feel hard. What, if anything, about silence makes you uncomfortable? Take a moment to pray over your concerns, remembering that Jesus meets each one with gentleness and compassion.

What do we learn about God's character from his invitation into silence?

Prayer

Jesus, you are the Prince of Peace. In you there is no confusion or chaos. I am surrounded by noise and often sucked into it. Thank you for providing pockets of quiet in which to still my soul. I'm so grateful that you speak to me in the ordinary moments of my day. Help me to look for those pockets of silence. Please meet me there and help me to listen for your voice.

Digging Deeper into Silence

If you have bonus time, I invite you to explore an additional passage on silence. Write out Isaiah 26:3-4 on an index card or Post-it so you can refer to it throughout your week.

Now let's take some time to look deeply at Isaiah 26:3-4. We want to see this passage in its context, understand the words used, and discover its meaning.

How would you express the idea of this passage in your own words?

You will keep the mind that
is dependent on you
in perfect peace,
for it is trusting in you.
Trust in the LORD forever,
because in the LORD,
the LORD himself, is an
everlasting rock!

ISAIAH 26:3-4

What are the key words? What do they mean?

How does God describe himself in this passage?

A SECOND LOOK AT Silence

The spring air rushed into my face as I biked as hard as my legs could move. The blood rushed through my body, and my breath bloomed tight in my chest. I rounded the corner and brought my bike to a stop. The grass was just coming in over the slope down to the creek. The trees with freshly budding leaves bent to touch the edges of the water.

I leaned my bike against the guardrail and wandered out to the center of the bridge. I sat there, legs dangling over the edge. I listened to the bubbling of the water over the rocks all through the middle of the river. The golden beams of light filtering through the leaves cast distinct rays that sparkled on the rivulets of water. After a while, the direction of the light changed, and the spell was broken. I hopped back on my bike and slowly made my way home, storing that memory in my heart.

Several years later, I was living in the city and close to a breakdown. The work environment I had landed in was harsh and critical, and I didn't have a church support or anyone to comfort me in it. There in the middle of a crowded city dense with hot concrete and asphalt, I settled onto a step and played back that beautiful memory while quoting Psalm 62:5 to myself: "Rest in God alone, my soul, for my hope comes from him." In my loneliness and burnout, God refreshed me again through the memory of what he had created and what he had done in the past.

We often assume that we'll find peace only in the quiet moments of life. But the "perfect peace" described in Isaiah 26:3-4 doesn't come simply from the absence of noise or never talking but rather from focusing our minds on the one who is peace. We quickly lose our inner quiet when we have too much input without pausing to listen to the one who gives peace or when we talk too much, filling all the silences with our own thoughts. Because we live in an economy where attention is directly connected to money, many companies capitalize on our need for distraction from inner pain and trials. Social media, apps, and streaming services are designed to draw us in. Other ways we numb out include throwing ourselves into our next work project, talking during any uncomfortable silences, or losing ourselves in someone else's life drama.

We are reluctant to let go of these distractions because when we stop our work and turn off our TVs, music, and phones, we are left alone with our rattling thoughts. During an uncomfortable silence, all the things we've pushed down and covered with noise begin to rise to the surface. In the quiet, we are reminded of our fears. We worry that we will never be someone's special person, we recall the words our parents spoke to us in a low moment, or we become stuck in anxiety over a misspoken word.

As humans, we all have an internal hunger that we are trying to satisfy. We distract ourselves from this hunger when we spend long hours working, endlessly swipe through video content on social media, listen to podcast after podcast, or attend every social function life presents us with. But ultimately these things don't fill the innermost parts of our soul.

We long for something more because we were created to live in perfect relationship with God and one another, in a world without thorns and decay. Before the fall, work in the garden always led to more beauty. Yet we look around and that isn't our reality. We are living in a world that is broken. We jog to stay ahead of the housework, we get a diagnosis that changes our life, or we struggle to navigate a difficult relationship.

Without the cohesion of the gospel story, none of it adds up. Trying to make sense of it is enough to drive anyone mad, and so we numb out.

And yet amid this brokenness, Isaiah 26:3-4 offers a glimmer of hope: the promise of perfect peace. Isaiah is a prophetic book in the Old Testament. In the days of the Old Testament, God's people often told stories of those who had gone before them and witnessed God's faithfulness. Those stories provided an element of peace with the promise of a Savior who would come. But so much was still a mystery. Then Jesus came. He was the missing piece. The mystery was revealed in his life, death, resurrection, and promise to come again. He came to be God with us, and he didn't just redeem us and leave—he promised believers that the Holy Spirit would be God in us!

When we are surrendered to God, we don't have to continually distract ourselves. We have found rest with our Savior. On the cross, Jesus experienced ultimate restlessness so that we could find rest in him. Jesus transforms loneliness to peaceful solitude. If loneliness is defined as internal emptiness, then spiritual solitude is internal fullness.

This isn't to say that we should attempt to always be alone or never speak during conversation. There are pitfalls to both isolating ourselves and to constantly being in the company of others. If we are always alone, it's easy to get lost in the echo chamber of our own thoughts and self-interest. If we are constantly around others, we don't have the time or ability to listen to how the Holy Spirit would change our behaviors and interactions. We are called to be in community and serve.

It is only when we are gazing at God that we can truly find peace. The best way to do this is by reading the Word that he has left for us. When we are lost in the beauty of who he is, we can know who we are and how we should love our neighbor. This also equips us to better know when we should speak and when we should keep silent (James 3:1-12).

When we have spent time in silence with the one who gives peace, we can move forward into the noise without losing our connection to peace. We begin to identify the broken parts of our stories and find healing in the one who writes good stories. Things may not physically change for us, and we may still have the same set of problems. But knowing where we fit into the story—and knowing that one day God is bringing a Kingdom with no more tears—allows us to see the pain we are facing with the hope that this isn't the end of the story. The Author of Life is writing a story that ends with eternal perfect peace.

So today, look for small moments to keep your mind fixed on this truth and listen for the gentle voice of Jesus. As you do, you will experience the perfect peace of the one who daily tends your needs and transforms you to be more like him.

Additional Context

I've listed some more of my favorite passages on silence below. After reading each passage in your Bible, use the space provided to respond to one (or both) of these questions:

> **What does this teach you about how and why to practice silence?**
>
> **What does this reveal to you about who God is?**

You can also choose to simply write out the passage. Writing the Word of God helps solidify it in our hearts.

Psalm 131:2

Proverbs 17:28

Proverbs 18:13

James 1:19

A Second Invitation into Silence

Are there any areas of your life in which you especially need God's perfect peace? What are some ways you can invite God into those areas and practice silence this week?

God calls himself the "Prince of Peace" (Isaiah 9:6). How does this name change the way you see God?

Simplicity

Simplicity is when we give up being driven by what we possess. This allows us to love others better because when we don't have to spend hours maintaining our belongings and image, we have more time available to follow Christ's call to serve and love those around us.

Simplicity stands in contrast to both materialism and minimalism. Materialism is when we define ourselves by what we have, our reputation, and our status. And minimalism is when we are motivated to give up as much as possible, often out of a sense of moral superiority, which can lead to legalism (thinking Jesus loves us more if we perform well). It's easy to fall into the trap of using accumulation or reduction to prove ourselves to others rather than serving them in Christ's love. The biblical practice of simplicity helps us shift our focus from finding our worth in fleeting earthly possessions to investing in eternal things.

Video Notes

DISCUSSION AND REFLECTION QUESTIONS

- What are some ways you see materialism in everyday culture?
- Have you ever had a precious object broken by someone else? How did you respond? What does your response say about your relationship to "stuff"?
- What are some ways our possessions hold us captive?

To access the video session, use the instructions in the front of your Bible study book.

A Record of God's Gentle Tending

Sometimes we think God doesn't meet with us, when really we just don't pause long enough to notice what he's already doing. Take a moment to record how God is tending you.

Write down some of the people, things, or experiences that you're grateful for. How has God provided for your needs in a way that has allowed you to rest contentedly in him?

Finding Simplicity in the Word

Write out Matthew 6:19-21 on an index card or Post-it so you can refer to it throughout your week.

Now let's take some time to look deeply at Matthew 6:19-21. We want to see this passage in its context, understand the words used, and discover its meaning.

Compare and contrast the two approaches to life presented in this passage.

Don't store up for yourselves treasures on earth, where moth and rust destroy and where thieves break in and steal. But store up for yourselves treasures in heaven, where neither moth nor rust destroys, and where thieves don't break in and steal. For where your treasure is, there your heart will be also.

MATTHEW 6:19-21

How would you express the idea of this passage in your own words?

Matthew 6:24 helps us further understand the consequences of storing up treasures on earth. According to verse 24, what happens when we try to put both God and possessions at the center of our lives?

LET'S DIG INTO

Simplicity

"Where your treasure is, there your heart will be also," I quoted to myself as I swept up thirty-two shattered terra-cotta pots. My two toddlers had accidently knocked one over and realized what a lovely sound it made as it shattered. They spent the next fifteen minutes destroying the rest as I nursed our newborn baby and tried to get him to sleep in the back bedroom. When I stepped out and saw what they had done, tears filled my eyes. Their own eyes grew wide as they realized that the broken pots couldn't be snapped back together like LEGO bricks.

After the initial shock, I noticed peace creeping around the corners of my heart, and it surprised me. I had often become unbearably sad when things I loved got broken. At this point, with a house full of little boys, a lot of things got broken—not from carelessness, but from the ordinary everyday usage of a home that welcomed not just our own little people but those of friends we felt called to serve and host.

That day, I realized the reason I could face this newest shattering of things I loved was because for years God had been weaning me of extra love for the things of this world. I learned to release my hold on earthly possessions in the days I worked with kids and my car had been accidentally scratched. I learned this lesson again when I had to throw away a favorite shirt that was stained by the bleach we used to sanitize tables before passing out meals at the food bank.

Possessions, when used for God's glory, are sacrifices to him for Kingdom work. And when they are used up for his glory, they are not wasted.

I would love to say this became my attitude from then on, but my kids can testify that is not the case. Culture tells me that my things are a way for me to increase my status and reputation, and it's a constant battle to see things the way God sees them.

We live in a world that is constantly pointing out what we don't have. You can't drive from one place to another without seeing billboards that promise happiness or fulfillment. Turning on the TV or our phones puts sound to those ads. We can even be tempted to place too much value on possessions when we hear our friends talk about what they just purchased or the next trip they plan to take. The writer of Ecclesiastes 7:29 points out that God made people to be without corruption, but we often turn away from his good design to pursue complicated plans and inventions of our own devising.

We wrap our identity around the way we decorate our houses, the vacations we take, the clothes we wear, or the cars we drive. We confidently walk into a room in the right shoes or the correct shade of lipstick, believing that it changes the way we will be received by others (and in some ways, we aren't wrong). We are constantly assessing others to see if they measure up to the group values. We panic when asked to host a baby shower, fearing that we won't meet all the expectations. Or maybe we are the first to volunteer, because we know we can nail it and crave the attention. All this pressure weighs on our hearts and minds.

But Jesus reminds us in Matthew 6:19-21 that we don't have to be caught up in the endless pursuit of status and possessions. This passage in Matthew is centered directly in the middle of one of Jesus' most renowned teachings during his earthly ministry: the Sermon on the Mount. In it he lays out what he values as well as why he came—to save us and help us live in alignment with his Kingdom.

Sin first entered the world when humans rebelled against God and took what they thought was best for them. This resulted in their loss of direct communication with God. When they were no longer able to walk with God in the garden of Eden, their purpose became lost and fuzzy. Rather than knowing deep down that they were created for beauty and the enjoyment of God and one another, they became trapped in the constant struggle to possess more and outdo each other. After the fall, Adam and Eve realized they were naked, felt shame, and attempted to cover themselves. Not long after this, the first murder was committed by Cain against his brother Abel. Cain was jealous that God accepted Abel's offering but rejected his own, so he attempted to cover his shame by removing the one who was doing better.

Jesus' descent from heaven to earth completely upended the priority system of being the best. He left streets of gold and the riches of heaven to redeem his people. He emptied himself to wear the likeness of humanity (Philippians 2:7). He ate with society's outcasts and healed people who would have been uncultured and in the shadows of society. Then he died, stripped of his clothes in front of the crowds so that we might be clothed in his righteousness.

Now we live with the promise of salvation, which allows us to release our hold on earthly treasures to invest in things of eternal importance. The idea of devaluing "stuff" may remind you of that minimalism book you read a few years ago, but Christian simplicity has a different internal motivation than minimalism. While minimalism is often motivated by a sense of moral superiority that leads to legalism or performance-based faith, Christian simplicity is grounded in our secure identity in Christ. We live in the truth that we are bought with a price and freed from shame. We don't need to prove ourselves by giving up as much as possible.

Similarly, Christian simplicity stands in opposition to materialism, where we attempt to define ourselves by accumulating more. The gospel reminds us that we are not defined by what we have, our reputation, or our status. Our goal is not to impress others but rather to serve them in Christ's love.

When we give up being driven by what we possess, it frees us to love better. When we don't have to spend hours maintaining our belongings, we have more time available to follow Christ's call to serve and love others.

To live simply is also to live in faith that what we need will be provided for us. Jesus teaches in Matthew 6:25-29 that we shouldn't worry about our lives—what we will eat, drink, or wear—because we are held and cared for by our Savior.

The goal of simplicity isn't to live in forced poverty. God made creation good and wants it to be enjoyed. We can enjoy beauty without becoming defined by what we own. We don't live simply to show how much we love God but to "seek first the kingdom of God and his righteousness," and all we need will be provided for us (Matthew 6:33).

When we understand the extent of Christ's love for us, it's easier for us to find our value in what he thinks about us rather than what we have. Then the things the world views as important begin to not matter much at all. When we recognize that he is the one who gives us good gifts and happiness, we don't have to try to find our happiness in the latest dopamine hit from a shopping spree.

We don't have to perform to find favor with God, either by gathering things to give us status or giving them up to be more righteous. He has already given us everything we need for life and godliness in Jesus (2 Peter 1:3). What we do need to do is spend time with him. In doing that, what matters to him will start to matter to us.

In Context

I've listed some of my favorite passages on simplicity below. After reading each passage in your Bible, use the space provided to respond to one (or both) of these questions:

> **What does this teach you about how and why to practice simplicity?**
>
> **What does this reveal to you about who God is?**

You can also choose to simply write out the passage. Writing the Word of God helps solidify it in our hearts.

Philippians 2:7

Matthew 6:25-33

2 Peter 1:3

1 Timothy 6:6-7

A Gentle Invitation into Simplicity

What are some ways you try to prove yourself or find your worth and security in possessions? How can you invite God to help you invest in eternal things this week?

What do you sense God might be calling you to do with your money or possessions?

Prayer

God, through you I have not only everything I need, but the promise of eternity with you. I often live as if this life is all there is, and I need to get everything I can out of it. Thank you for inviting my soul into rest and contentment. Thank you for providing an identity where I'm loved outside of what I have or can do. Help that reality to sink deeply into my soul. Help me to remember that I am loved and have worth because I'm made in your image.

Digging Deeper into Simplicity

If you have bonus time, I invite you to explore an additional verse on simplicity. Write out Hebrews 13:5 on an index card or Post-it so you can refer to it throughout your week.

> Now let's take some time to look deeply at Hebrews 13:5. We want to see this verse in its context, understand the words used, and discover its meaning.

What are the two lifestyles mentioned?

Keep your life free from the love of money. Be satisfied with what you have, for he himself has said, I will never leave you or abandon you.

HEBREWS 13:5

What is the promise given to us in this verse?

The promise found in Hebrews 13:5 is also given in Deuteronomy 31:8. What does this repetition reveal to us about God's character and promises across generations?

A SECOND LOOK AT

Simplicity

Not long after having a home of my own I realized how hard it was going to be to own only what we needed rather than collecting what was available.

I grew up in a rural area with parents who embraced a life of simplicity to serve others. Then I moved to a city where every corner had a garage sale offering more items than we could realistically store, available for just a few dollars. I bought so much stuff. Soon I was overwhelmed with how much time I had to spend organizing and cleaning.

To counter this, I took a yearlong fast from buying myself any new clothes. Then I progressed to only buying things to replace what had become worn out and, if at all possible, only buying from secondhand stores. Finally, I settled on keeping in my closet only what I could hang on twenty-five hangers.

Each year I took this lifestyle to a new level until I discovered the zero-waste lifestyle and attempted to reduce our waste to a quart of trash per month. (The ultimate goal was to get down to a quart per year.) I attacked our trash with the zeal of a missionary.

After a few months had passed, I realized that what had begun with good intentions was turning into something ugly in my heart. One night we had friends over for dinner, as we often did, and when they came, they brought with them a dessert wrapped in a very not-compostable package. The second they walked in the door, my heart rate surged, and internally I went into a full-blown panic. What was I going to do with that trash? It didn't fit into my compost bin.

I know I seemed "off" the rest of that night, because I couldn't stop thinking about what I was going to do with the trash. I knew I couldn't send my friends out the door with the trash they brought, but at the same time, keeping it would ruin my plan.

Later that evening, while I was lying in bed, God spoke to my heart and reminded me that the ultimate call on my life was to serve, not to live simply. I had allowed a good thing to become an ultimate thing and had turned a calling into legalism.

Neither people who hoard nor those who give up everything have freedom. At its core, simplicity isn't about having possessions or not having them, making a ton of trash or barely any at all. It's about what our heart is focusing on.

Today's Scripture verse, Hebrews 13:5, is part of a series of instructions in Hebrews 13 that shows Christians how to live in the freedom Christ brings. It doesn't say "live a life free of money." It doesn't say "never buy another thing." It says be free from the *love* of money.

We've all known people who are obsessed with the things they have. Some rack up thousands of dollars of credit card debt to create an image. Others work out nonstop to be able to show up with the perfect body. Many become upset when their stuff gets broken.

As Christians, we don't have to be obsessed with what we have because we have "God with us" (Matthew 1:23, ESV). But how does the promise that God "will never leave you or abandon you" (Hebrews 13:5) serve as the antidote to our obsession with possessions? To understand the depth of this promise, we have to go back to the story of creation.

Adam and Eve walked and talked with God in the garden. They didn't feel shame even with nothing in their hands, standing naked before God and each other. But when brokenness entered the world through sin, shame is the first side effect mentioned. Humanity's first action after sin entered the world was to attempt to cover their shame and hide.

Most of us hide behind the things we own, our titles, or our relationships. But Jesus didn't want to leave us alone in our shame, so he came to be "God with us." He was born to the virgin Mary, he lived and taught among us, and then he sacrificed his life to pay for our sins. On the cross, he was stripped naked and brought through the throes of death in public view while taking every sin onto his head. He fully took all our shame onto himself so we can stand confident in his love. After he ascended into heaven, he sent the Holy Spirit to be God in us (2 Corinthians 6:16).

Knowing deep down that Jesus loves us and has covered our shame enables us to trust him to care for us and our things. We can still take wise precautions, such as having a savings account or buying insurance, but we balance this with the truth that "the LORD gives, and the LORD takes away. Blessed be the name of the LORD" (Job 1:21).

When we open our hands in generosity to share what we have with others, it frees us. That generosity signals to our hearts that "you are not your own, for you were bought at a price" (1 Corinthians 6:19-20). We can share freely with others, knowing that if a time of need arises, we can cast our cares on the one who cares for us (1 Peter 5:7).

This heart change doesn't just stay inside. Yes, the first step of transformation begins in our hearts, but what's in our hearts should overflow into our actions. If we know we are cared for by God, we don't have to grab as much as we can to feel secure and cared for. If our soul has been freed by knowing whose we are, we can trust God to take care of our needs. This allows us to release our anxiety about planning for every possible threat. If we believe all we have has been given to us, we will experience the peace of God as we give it away. This is markedly different from someone who believes they have things because they have worked hard for them, or who believes they can maintain what they have by their own intelligence.

God has already provided for us the fundamentals of life—air, water, and sun, as well as love, friendship, and salvation. You are released to live in freedom! Maybe this means you go and buy the sweater. Or you choose to drive an old car. Is God calling you to give up shopping for a few weeks or months? Pray that he reveals to you where your treasure is so that he can realign your love as you remember the truth that he has removed your shame and will never leave you.

Additional Context

I've listed some more of my favorite passages on simplicity below. After reading each passage in your Bible, use the space provided to respond to one (or both) of these questions:

What does this show you about how to practice simplicity?

What does this reveal to you about who God is?

You can also choose to simply write out the passage. Writing the Word of God helps solidify it in our hearts.

Ecclesiastes 5:10

Luke 12:15

2 Corinthians 4:18

1 Timothy 6:7-8

A Second Invitation into Simplicity

Is there a habit God is calling you to start or something he's calling you to give up?

Is there something that this lesson on simplicity inspires you to pray for?

Gently Tending

Your Life in Community

You are created in the image of a triune God who lives continually in eternal harmony with himself as Father, Son, and Spirit. He designed people to live in community with him and with one another. You aren't meant to be alone. Living in community presents blessings, challenges, and so many beautiful ways to grow more fruit of the Spirit in your life. As you engage with the following spiritual disciplines, ask God to guide you in your relationships. These are the practices that will equip you to better reflect the harmony of the Trinity within your community.

Confession

Confession isn't simply regret or grief for having done wrong. Confession is realizing what you've done with remorse, believing Jesus' work and grace cover your sins, and then fighting for active change in your life.[22]

Video Notes

DISCUSSION AND REFLECTION QUESTIONS

- Describe a scene from a movie or book where the villain confesses. How did it make you feel? Did it teach you anything? Did you feel like their confession would lead to change?
- What elements do you think are needed in a good confession so you know change will happen?
- The word *confess* usually carries negative feelings. Can you think of a context in which it's used in a positive way?

To access the video session, use the instructions in the front of your Bible study book.

A Record of God's Gentle Tending

Sometimes we think God doesn't meet with us, when really we just don't pause long enough to notice what he's already doing. Take a moment to record how God is tending you.

Do you have people in your life with whom you can honestly share your struggles and trust to hold the tender places of your heart? Who are they, and what makes you able to open up to them?

Finding Confession in the Word

Write out 1 John 1:9 on an index card or Post-it so you can refer to it throughout your week.

Now let's take some time to look deeply at 1 John 1:9. We want to see this verse in its context, understand the words used, and discover its meaning.

What descriptive words are used for God in this verse?

If we confess our sins, he is faithful and righteous to forgive us our sins and to cleanse us from all unrighteousness.

1 JOHN 1:9

What does this verse say God does when we confess?

Look up the definition of *confess* in the dictionary. What key words stand out to you?

LET'S DIG INTO

Confession

I lay in bed, my mind racing. I reached over to pick up my phone and check the time. It was 1:07 a.m. *Gah, only six more hours to sleep*—and that was optimistic. I set my phone down gently, hoping not to wake my husband, who was snoring beside me.

I flipped my pillow to the cool side and closed my eyes, determined to fall asleep. All the clichés say that counting sheep helps people fall asleep. Desperate, I tried picturing a fluffy lamb jumping over the fence. But unbidden, into my mind came the conversation from the previous evening.

My cheeks flushed with shame as I thought about the joke that I took too far, the way I defended myself and cared more about winning the debate than the feelings of my guests.

The familiar knot wound itself back in the pit of my stomach, and I started mapping out all the ways I could have handled the conversation better. I wished that I could hop in a time machine to rewrite the past. Now that I was caught in a shame spiral, everything embarrassing I had ever said or done started to pop into my head.

The next day I texted an apology to the friend I had joked about. She called back saying she appreciated that I was willing to apologize, but I hadn't offended her. If I had chosen to hide my shame, I would have continued to spiral rather than being known, forgiven, and loved. There have been many other times, though, when my apology for real sin and seeking forgiveness for harm done was needed. Regardless of the outcome, confession has always brought freedom.

Maybe the first time you read today's verse, 1 John 1:9, you froze, because the idea of saying aloud the ways you have failed to a perfect God makes your shame feel overwhelming.

This verse wasn't included in the Bible to make us to feel shame, but rather to experience freedom.

Before the death of Jesus, sin was forgiven by confessing in the Temple. God's people were required to bring a lamb or smaller animal that would be killed to atone for their sin. This confession was public, time-consuming, expensive, and bloody. But after Jesus became the ultimate atoning sacrifice for us on the cross, this process was no longer necessary.

First John was written to people who lived while Jesus walked the earth. John's audience would have been familiar with Jesus' life, death, and resurrection. In 1 John 1:9, John is reminding the early church that they have direct access to God. Jesus took our shame so that we can come to God as his beloved children. Our shame has been crucified with Christ.

From John 3:16, we know that when Jesus died on the cross, his payment for sin wasn't done in anger but in love. God doesn't grudgingly forgive us; he is and always has been eagerly willing to do whatever it takes to restore relationship with us—even when that meant taking all of humanity's wrongdoing into his own body. He was willing to fully identify with human pain and suffering and experience alienation from God to defeat death and darkness (Philippians 2:6-8).

What a beautiful thing it is to remember that God doesn't come at our failings with a hammer, ready to pound out our sin. Instead, he gently invites us back into his presence with open hands—hands scarred by the nail holes from the work he already did for us on the cross. Work that was given freely. He eagerly moved into relationship with us. As believers, our sin and brokenness don't need to drive us into the pit of self-condemnation and shame. Instead, we can lift our heart and eyes to the one who walked through shame on the cross to neutralize the power of sin and shame over us. Jesus told us that he is like the father of the prodigal son who saw his rebellious child far off in the distance and ran with joy to welcome him back home.

When we come into the embrace of our Savior and spend meaningful time with God, our soul feels his presence. We become aware of what we have done and what we have left undone.[23] We become itchy and uncomfortable engaging in sinful behaviors that used to be normal. At this point, we have a choice to make. We can attempt to justify our actions or move to busyness to rid ourselves of discomfort. Busyness causes the negative feelings to subside, but by busying ourselves, we may quench the conviction of the Holy Spirit rather than being transformed by it (1 Thessalonians 5:19). A third—and better—choice is confession.

Confession isn't simply the regret or grief for having done wrong. Confession comes in three steps:

- realizing what you've done with remorse,
- believing that Jesus' work and grace cover your sins, and then
- fighting for active change in your life.[24]

Growth results when we realize we can come to Jesus and tell him all our sins. He already sees and knows them anyway.

Some of us were taught to picture God as a judge who is ready to condemn us if we don't say the exact right words of confession to unlock the cell of shame and escape punishment. But even in the Old Testament, the heart of God's character is a desire to forgive and a huge capacity for love. Numerous times throughout the Old Testament God repeats, nearly word for word, that he is merciful, compassionate, slow to anger, and filled with unfailing love (Exodus 34:6; Numbers 14:18; Psalm 86:5; and Psalm 103:8).

If you've started to worry that you will miss one of the steps in confession, remember that God is the one who is moving your heart to desire forgiveness. He is your loving, kind Father who is kneeling before you with open arms ready to receive you. He is also the compassionate Shepherd, the one who ran to find you before you knew you were lost. On the cross, he reached into danger to rescue you from it. Now he prompts you to confess so you can be released from the natural shame that comes with being human after the fall, and he teaches you step-by-step how to live free.

In Context

I've listed some of my favorite passages on confession below. After reading each passage in your Bible, use the space provided to respond to one (or both) of these questions:

What does this teach you about how and why to practice confession?

What does this reveal to you about who God is?

You can also choose to simply write out the passage. Writing the Word of God helps solidify it in our hearts.

Proverbs 28:13

John 20:23

Romans 10:9-11

Psalm 32:5-6

A Gentle Invitation into Confession

As you've learned more about the discipline of confession, do you sense the Holy Spirit nudging you to confess anything to God?

Recall the three steps of confession: realizing what you've done with remorse, admitting your sin honestly before God, and then moving into active life change. Which of these three steps is hardest for you, and why? Ask the Holy Spirit to help you grow in this area.

Prayer

Lord, you are so faithful and righteous. Even before I asked, you promised to forgive and cleanse me from my sin. I struggle to confess sin, often feeling like you couldn't possibly forgive me.

Thank you for sending your Son to pay for my sin so that I can come to you openly. Help me to see your love more every day so that I run to you with my confession instead of offering it anxiously or grudgingly.

Digging Deeper into Confession

If you have bonus time, I invite you to explore an additional verse on confession. Write out James 5:16 on an index card or Post-it so you can refer to it throughout your week.

Now let's take some time to look deeply at James 5:16. We want to see this verse in its context, understand the words used, and discover its meaning.

What is an important practice for believers we are taught about here?

Confess your sins to one another and pray for one another, so that you may be healed. The prayer of a righteous person is very powerful in its effect.

JAMES 5:16

What is the result of confession and prayer? What do you think that would look like in your life?

Can you think of any stories from the Old Testament where God's people practiced confession? What do you learn from these examples? (If you can't think of an example, see Psalm 51.)

A SECOND LOOK AT

Confession

Confession doesn't come easily. I don't know if that's just a "me" thing or if our whole culture struggles with it, but regardless, I find that this practice requires some extra effort.

A little over a year ago, my husband and I were asked to take leadership of our community group when the previous leaders moved cross-country. After a bit of hesitation and a lot of prayer, we agreed. But if I had known ahead of time what my role would entail, I might have asked to pass on the opportunity . . .

Every month, I was to gather with the women of our group for intentional discipleship time. We were provided a list of questions to cover to deepen our spiritual walk and draw us closer to Christ:

1. What did you read in the Bible that you're applying to your life?
2. How is God changing you to be more like him?
3. What's been hard in your life lately?
4. Are there any sins or temptations you need to confess?
5. Who are you building a relationship with who doesn't already know Jesus?

I got to question four and heard a record scratch in my mind . . .

I'm sorry, *what?!*

I'm supposed to go in and ask these other grown-up women what sin they need to confess? I think I'll just skip that part, thanks.

During our first group meeting, we all sat down to dinner and started chatting. We covered the first three questions on the list, and then I skipped to the last. One of the women spoke up quietly and asked if I hadn't skipped a question. I'm confident I turned beet red.

I cleared my throat and read the question. She offered to go first, and then we all went. By the time we were done, I was crying a bit, but I felt the presence of Jesus and the hope of the gospel in a way I hadn't for a while—and to think I had almost skipped over that question!

James 5:16 gives us a template for what confession looks like in community. Remember that James was one of the earliest New Testament books written. It's oddly comforting to realize that from the beginning, Christians have sinned against one another and needed to confess to one another. The church isn't perfect, and we often struggle to follow God's ways, but we've been bought at a price (1 Corinthians 6:20). Christ's sacrifice makes a way for us to live in alignment with Christ's new Kingdom. As we grow to become more like him, it's important that we not only take time for personal confession of our shortcomings but also acknowledge our sin in a group to experience the healing and freedom that Christ offers.

In my church, there is a time of silence during the service when we're invited to privately confess our sins, and then we confess our sins together as a congregation through corporate recitations. These readings are usually centuries old, passed down through the church over generations, and they often remind us of sins that have become so culturally normalized that it's easy to overlook the ways they show up in our lives each day.

At first, these times of confession made me feel itchy and uncomfortable. It seemed as if everyone around me could read the guilt on my face as I prayed. But gradually I came to see how these prayers actually level the playing field, because every other person in the congregation recites the same confession along with me. People who are brand-new to faith and people who have been Christians for fifty years all need forgiveness.

At the very end of the recitation, while we're feeling at our lowest, the leader steps forward to remind us of truth. His tone rises in excitement as the story unfolds: "You were bought at a price and are not under condemnation and shame from God. Because of Jesus' perfect life and sacrificial death, you can lift your hearts to the Lord." Faces that were so serious before often soften into smiles as we cry out with joy together, "Thanks be to God."

Not only does confession in community help us see the church's shared need of a Savior, but it can also help us move beyond our heavy burden of guilt. *The Book of Common Prayer* is a historic liturgical text that notes how confessing our sins to a fellow believer can point us to healing in Christ. Paraphrased, it says, "If your conscience won't be quiet, then tell your grief to another believer and allow them to counsel or comfort you."[25]

Some of us carry too much guilt. If we open ourselves to talking about it with other believers, they can remind us of the truth of the gospel. The goal of confessing our sin to another believer isn't that they will forgive us. Instead, it helps us remind each other that Jesus came to forgive our sins. He knew that every human was a sinner and that even after his sacrifice on the cross, we would fail again. But he loved us in spite of our failures, and because he rose from the dead we are not under the condemnation of God. He crushed the shame that sin brings and loosed the bonds of guilt forever. So we are free to find relief in confession and move forward to live in the smile of his love.

James 5:16 encourages us that when we confess our sins to one another, we can experience healing and peace. But as you do this, exercise wisdom. Some Christians won't have enough maturity or empathy to point you back to the gospel. Others may either think that what you've done isn't too bad or be shocked and horrified. If you don't know whom to choose to be your accountability partner, pray and ask the Holy Spirit to guide you in finding a trustworthy friend who is wise and gentle.

On the flip side, you can aim to be a soft place to land for someone who needs to confess. We who have experienced the mercy and grace of Jesus can extend that kindness to others. One of the hardest things to learn is how to listen in silence—not to go off on your own story of something you did that was similar or relieve the awkwardness by making a joke, but to genuinely listen. Don't pry for more than God is leading the other person to share, but quietly give space to hear them. You might even silently pray for them as you hear the pain that they are revealing to you. Finally, remind them of the work that Christ has done to release them from shame and into joy. Pray with them at the end of your time together.

Continue to carry their concerns to God in prayer over the next week. Ask God to help them find healing as they move to actively fight against sin. Be sure to check in with them as it feels appropriate or send a verse that feels applicable to the situation.

The beauty of confession is that it releases us from having to pretend to be someone we aren't. We can be seen, known, and loved as we are in the body of Christ. This ability to be honest allows us to live changed lives.

Additional Context

I've listed some more of my favorite passages on confession below. After reading each passage in your Bible, use the space provided to respond to one (or both) of these questions:

> **What does this teach you about how and why to practice confession?**
>
> **What does this reveal to you about who God is?**

You can also choose to simply write out the passage. Writing the Word of God helps solidify it in our hearts.

Matthew 3:6

Acts 19:18

Romans 10:10

Leviticus 5:5

A Second Invitation into Confession

What are some things you carry guilt over that you need to let go of in light of God's forgiveness?

How would practicing confession change the way you live?

Stewardship

Stewardship is recognizing that our time, money, resources, and relationships come from God. We use them the way that he directs, believing that he knows best what to do with the gifts he has given us. We don't obsessively try to control all we have, but we also don't frivolously waste it, because we know that it's a beautiful gift from God to be used for our good and his glory.

Video Notes

DISCUSSION AND REFLECTION QUESTIONS

- Do you know someone who stewards their money or resources well? What makes them an effective steward?
- What makes stewardship of your time hard? What can be an obstacle to stewarding your time well?
- Are different skills needed to steward relationships well?

To access the video session, use the instructions in the front of your Bible study book.

A Record of God's Gentle Tending

Sometimes we think God doesn't meet with us, when really we just don't pause long enough to notice what he's already doing. Take a moment to record how God is tending you.

What routines and habits have helped you use your time, money, resources, and relationships well? Who taught you to do those things?

Finding Stewardship in the Word

Write out 1 Peter 4:10 on an index card or Post-it so you can refer to it throughout your week.

Now let's take some time to look deeply at 1 Peter 4:10. We want to see this verse in its context, understand the words used, and discover its meaning.

This verse notes that we each have received a gift. What kind of "gifts" is this verse referring to?

Just as each one has received a gift, use it to serve others, as good stewards of the varied grace of God.

1 PETER 4:10

What does this verse call us to do with the gift we've received? What might that involve?

Write this verse into a prayer, including the specific gifts you know God has given you.

LET'S DIG INTO

Stewardship

My breath tightened in my chest as I called for my boys to put on their shoes and head to the car. Glancing around the house, my anxiety spiked further as I spotted egg dried on the countertop and piles of books and toys filling our entryway. Everything inside of me wanted to stay and tidy our house, which was cluttered by the ordinary chaos of life with small children. But today I knew God was asking me to go help someone else. So we would go and serve. Then, when I came home, I would attempt to faithfully steward my space too.

Are you crazy, going to help someone else with laundry when your own house looks like this? I asked myself. I cringed, but off we drove.

Three hours later we banged our way back into the house with shoes, bags, and boy bodies. My husband was in the kitchen making lunch for us, and as I looked around I realized that he had cleared off several of the surfaces I'd been worried about. An hour later our babysitter arrived and helped me clean before she took off on an outing with the boys.

God knew the limitations of my own time and, through the gift of many helping hands, expanded what could be accomplished—far beyond anything I could've done if I had stayed home alone. I had been tempted in the moment to spiritualize ignoring the call to serve by saying that I was just trying to steward my time first. But ultimately I chose obedience.

When I said yes, it felt like the miracle of the loaves and the fish: My time was divided, blessed, and expanded. Finite resources, when turned over to the God of the universe, can be multiplied supernaturally to become infinitely more than what we can imagine or ask for.

In today's verse, 1 Peter 4:10, Peter encourages believers to faithfully steward their God-given gifts. First Peter, written during Peter's captivity in Rome, is addressed to people who were experiencing growing hostility from their communities. These early Christians had priorities and values that set them at odds with their friends, coworkers, government, and even family members. Peter's letter served as a guide for how to live out their faith among people who not only didn't understand it but openly opposed it.

The people around them were baffled that these Christians weren't interested in sleeping around, becoming drunk, participating in orgies, and cheating their way into better financial situations. Peter reminded them that they were to exhibit self-control, remain sober, and be full of prayer and love that brings forgiveness.

They were told to use the life and suffering of Christ as their inspiration. And to use their gifts well by serving others and offering hospitality without grumbling. In this way, they would be good stewards of God's grace.

The term *gifts* in 1 Peter 4:10 is often interpreted as "spiritual gifts," like those we find in 1 Corinthians 12:4-11. But in a broader sense, the term can also include all the resources and opportunities God has given us to steward. One God-given gift I often find challenging to steward well—especially in a culture filled with distraction and busyness—is my time.

Time management isn't an idea that started with the rise of self-help books; the Bible spoke about this issue long before that. We are told in Ephesians, "Pay careful attention, then, to how you walk . . . making the most of the time" (5:15-16). We see this same idea expressed in an Old Testament prayer: "Teach us to number our days carefully so that we may develop wisdom in our hearts" (Psalm 90:12). And we see it again in Proverbs: "Don't boast about tomorrow, for you don't know what a day might bring" (27:1). You don't have to read for long in the Bible to realize that time is seen as a valuable gift we are encouraged to treasure. We are called to steward it faithfully, but we also must remember that we can't predict what our future holds—our time is in God's hands.

There are two primary ways we can use our time poorly. One is to waste it. Believing we have plenty of time, we fill our days with drinking, partying, or doomscrolling—after all, we always have tomorrow to do what we should do. On the other end of the spectrum, we can be tempted to obsess over how every minute is spent, allowing time optimization to become a god. Inevitably, the god of time optimization will fail us.

It's easy to see how today's culture encourages our tendencies toward either waste or hyperproductivity. Those of us who have seen the "Are you still watching?" message come up on the TV after a binge know that there are endless hours of online streaming available. Algorithms are optimized to keep us scrolling longer. Online gaming has been engineered to foster addiction.

On the flip side, the productivity software industry alone is worth over eighty billion dollars.[26] Not to mention the billions in revenue that come from books, conferences, and training programs designed to aid individuals and companies in maximizing their time and productivity. We map out our daily routine for maximum efficiency and then guard it against anyone who would interrupt it with their needs.

If we are tempted to waste or optimize our time, Scripture has good news for us: "You are not your own, for you were bought at a price. So glorify God with your body" (1 Corinthians 6:19-20). Jesus' death was the ultimate gift of time. Our days were only numbered because of the fall. He chose to remove himself from his eternal nature to live a limited life in order to give us eternal life. We value the number of our days here because they were purchased by his precious blood, but we don't grip them too dearly because he paid for us to have new life eternally.

The reason we give up our time to serve others is that we are called to share in the work of Christ. Jesus' death didn't just provide the promise of heaven, though we do look forward to that. He died so that we can actively participate in his Kingdom now. When we serve, we see what a community united in love for Christ looks like. That is truly a glorious sight!

As people who were bought at a price, love motivates our plans. Throughout the New Testament, we are told repeatedly to love one another and to let others know us as Christians by our love. Stewarding our time well means spending our time on others. According to the theology of Martin Luther, the father of the Reformation, "God does not need our good works, but our neighbor does."[27]

We steward our God-given gifts to love people well because people are made in the image of God. They are loved by Jesus so much that he gave his life for them. And we are to follow Jesus' example. Some ways we might steward our gifts well include putting our phones down to look into the eyes of a friend, turning off the video games to play with our kids, and closing social media to clean a family member's house. Perhaps stewardship looks like shutting off the TV to pray for our neighbor who is battling cancer or leaving the comfort of our homes to feed the homeless or raise money for disaster relief.

When we remember that God is the one who is numbering our days, we find ourselves proactively bringing his good and light into the world. Bringing his love and good to others is the strongest way to combat sin in the world. Everything we do—the love we pour out, the service we give—isn't to make God love us more but because he first loved us (1 John 4:19). We can show the world through our good works what the promised new Kingdom will look like—a Kingdom under the reign of a God who is "slow to anger and abounding in faithful love and truth" (Exodus 34:6). How beautiful it is to be caught up in that mission, one with a promise of new mercies every morning (Lamentations 3:22-23).

So how is your story caught up in his story through stewardship? What does it look like to "glorify God with your body" (1 Corinthians 6:20)? Maybe your body is ravaged by illness, and your energy is limited. Can you smile and reply with gentleness when you would rather snap? Can you take a meal to a friend or invite someone in? As you offer your presence and give up your time and resources, I trust that you will find yourself gently tended by the Shepherd.

In Context

I've listed some of my favorite passages on stewardship below. After reading each passage in your Bible, use the space provided to respond to one (or both) of these questions:

What does this teach you about how and why to practice stewardship?

What does this reveal to you about who God is?

You can also choose to simply write out the passage. Writing the Word of God helps solidify it in our hearts.

2 Corinthians 9:7

Ephesians 5:15-16

Psalm 90:12

Proverbs 27:1

A Gentle Invitation into Stewardship

What gifts and strengths do you have that you know God wants to use?

What is something in your life God is leading you to steward for his glory?

Prayer

Lord, everything I have is from you, and you give good gifts. I often think that I make my own good gifts, and I forget to be grateful for and generous with what I have. Thank you for not loving me based on how well I steward my gifts, but please put in me a heart of generosity today.

Digging Deeper into Stewardship

If you have bonus time, I invite you to explore an additional passage on stewardship. Write out 2 Corinthians 9:6-7 on an index card or Post-it so you can refer to it throughout your week.

Now let's take some time to look deeply at 2 Corinthians 9:6-7. We want to see this passage in its context, understand the words used, and discover its meaning.

What words are repeated in these verses? What does the repetition emphasize?

The person who sows sparingly will also reap sparingly, and the person who sows generously will also reap generously. Each person should do as he has decided in his heart—not reluctantly or out of compulsion, since God loves a cheerful giver.

2 CORINTHIANS 9:6-7

Describe the two types of givers mentioned in this passage.

What is promised in this passage?

A SECOND LOOK AT

Stewardship

I sat in the dark nursery rocking the baby to sleep and listening to distant squeals of joy. I was baffled because when I had left the family room only ten minutes ago, my husband was reading a missionary story to our boys—enjoyable, but not usually the source of this level of delight. Curious, I lay the now-sleeping baby down and tiptoed out of the room.

One of the boys announced, "Mom, you'll never believe what happened in our story tonight! George Müller had a whole orphanage full of three hundred kids, but nothing to feed them. He used to be wealthy, but he gave away everything to help poor kids. He didn't even have one penny left, so he prayed and asked God to feed the kids. Right after that a baker knocked at the door, saying God woke him up that night and told him to bake three batches of bread. A few minutes later another guy knocked on the door and said his milk cart broke down. The milk was going to go bad, so he gave all the milk to the kids. It was more than enough for everyone! Even though George Müller didn't have money, he was happy as he watched the kids eat bread and drink milk until they were full."[28]

That evening as my husband and I talked, we realized that even though discipling our kids was one of the harder parts of parenting, we are often surprised by the joy that it brings. In our lives and in the life of George Müller, we see how faithfully stewarding our relationships can lead not only to amazing outcomes but our own joy as well.

Today's passage, 2 Corinthians 9:6-7, reminds us that "the person who sows generously will also reap generously." Because most of us are far removed from the agricultural world, this passage likely sounds more poetic than practical. In today's culture, we can wander through a supermarket and carefully select what to place in our carts. And if we forget something, we can often bop back over and pick it up. To understand what these verses meant to their original audience, we need to use our imagination and get into the mind of a farmer in the Roman Empire.

On a farm, you tend to get out of the ground what you put into it. A farmer in those days had to save seed from harvest the year before. All winter they had to decide how much to eat. Then in the spring he had to decide how much to plant and how much to save in case of emergency. He and his family still needed to have food over the summer, and there was always a chance that the first planting would wash out and he would have to start over.

Usually the first planting did fine. The more you planted, the larger your harvest would be and the more money you would make at harvest.

Paul is encouraging believers to not count the cost when investing in God's Kingdom work. While the focus of this verse is financial giving, the principle also extends to faithful stewardship of all our time, talents, and relationships. Especially when it comes to planting seeds of discipleship, we are instructed to not save back. You can put all your grain in the field, because when what we sow is given to God, the harvest is secure. We don't have to wonder if God is going to produce fruit in a life that is turned over to making disciples. In due season you *will* reap (Galatians 6:9)!

Especially for those who don't know Jesus and don't have the hope of eternity, it can be easy to live for the moment. There's a common saying: "Eat, drink, and be merry, for tomorrow we die." For our farming analogy, this might sound something like, "We won't be here in the fall to harvest anyway, so we might as well eat all the grain now." Many people spend all their money and resources on cars, trips, and the best experiences they can afford. After all, we just have this one wild, precious life to live.[29]

This mentality even creeps into the church. Rather than giving generously to those in need, we give only the minimum we feel is required. We show up to church on Sunday but still sleep with our boyfriend on Monday night, choosing temporary pleasure over lasting relationship. Or we may even try to get our kids into the best schools and tutoring programs, but at the cost of adequate time for discipling them.

The root of all these things is the same: We think we have to take what we are going to get out of life. We believe that we have to look out for ourselves first.

But when we read God's Word, talk to him, and live life with other believers, we start to see that our story is wrapped up in God's bigger story of creation, fall, redemption, and the new Kingdom to come. We come to know from experience that we can trust our Savior. We won't be called to anything that he won't meet us in. Jesus tells us that God is a good Father who cares for his children (Matthew 7:9) and will supply all our needs according to his riches (Philippians 4:19). Then, after we've tasted God's sustaining grace, we are inspired and empowered to generously share the gifts we have been given. We are brought into the new Kingdom, and we are given a desire to do anything we can to "go into all the world and preach the gospel" (Mark 16:15).

The basic fruit of coming to love Jesus is the longing to reach out and touch the lives of others. When we see how much knowing him has transformed us into healthy and vibrant people, we want others to experience that as well. We long for them to taste what it's like to live as a new creation (2 Corinthians 5:17).

As we reach out to love the way that Jesus loves, our relationship with him grows and flourishes. In other words, stewarding our relationships well is not just a result of our faith but also the fertilizer of our faith.

All believers are called to make new disciples. We tend to think that only older and more mature Christians can influence younger Christians. But in the Christian life, we are all walking hand in hand toward the new Kingdom. Without connection with new believers, our own faith becomes stale and dry. When seasoned believers explain the basics of the gospel to new Christians, it grows their own faith. The only way you truly know you've learned something is when you know it so well you can teach it to someone else.

As for the younger believers, without the wisdom of older believers, their faith may become unsteady and confused. We were created to be better together and participate in the bigger story of his Kingdom work.[30]

When we generously sow seeds of discipleship, our connection to the body of Christ is strengthened. The point is not to simply exchange information but to share life.

Today, I encourage you to assess how you're stewarding the relationships in your life. What might you feel called to lay down or give away to make disciples? Remember, God promises an abundant harvest to those who steward their gifts with open hands and generous hearts.

Additional Context

I've listed some more of my favorite passages on stewardship below. After reading each passage in your Bible, use the space provided to respond to one (or both) of these questions:

What does this teach you about how and why to practice stewardship?

What does this reveal to you about who God is?

You can also choose to simply write out the passage. Writing the Word of God helps solidify it in our hearts.

Matthew 28:19-20

Matthew 16:24

Mark 16:15

2 Timothy 4:2

A Second Invitation into Stewardship

How would your daily to-do list change if making disciples was your top priority?

What does God's delight in and prioritization of discipleship reveal to you about the love of God?

Worship

Worship is looking up and seeing something bigger and more beautiful than just ourselves and our own stories. It is those moments when we see who God really is and our hearts become overwhelmed with wonder and praise. When we spend time focusing on who God is and what his work looks like, we are better able to see his hand in our lives each day.

Video Notes

DISCUSSION AND REFLECTION QUESTIONS

- What is your go-to song when you're overjoyed?
- What are some nonmusical ways we can worship?
- How would you describe the difference between personal and communal worship?

To access the video session, use the instructions in the front of your Bible study book.

A Record of God's Gentle Tending

Sometimes we think God doesn't meet with us, when really we just don't pause long enough to notice what he's already doing. Take a moment to record how God is tending you.

Write down a moment when you saw how big God is and were overcome by worship. What led to that moment? What did you take away from that experience?

Finding Worship in the Word

Write out Psalm 95:6-7 on an index card or Post-it so you can refer to it throughout your week.

Now let's take some time to look deeply at Psalm 95:6-7. We want to see this passage in its context, understand the words used, and discover its meaning.

What are the different postures of worship noted in this passage?

Come, let's worship and
bow down;
let's kneel before
the Lord our Maker.
For he is our God,
and we are the people of
his pasture,
the sheep under his care.

PSALM 95:6-7

What inspires the psalmist to worship?

Can you think of other instances in the Bible where shepherd imagery is used? (If you can't think of an example, see John 10:1-18.)

LET'S DIG INTO

Worship

We hit a bump in the road, but even in the back seat of our van I hardly noticed. Deep in teen angst, I continued to scribble down all my thoughts on the page, until my dad's voice cut through my consciousness. "Sweetie, you should put your journal down. This is one of the most beautiful views in America." I rolled my eyes, sighed, folded my journal, and looked out the window.

Beside the road, small flowers were wrapped in foliage of dusty green-blue sitting at the base of enormous rocks and massive tree trunks. My eyes followed the rough bark up until I lost sight of the top when my eye hit the edge of the window frame. Suddenly, there was a break in the trees and towering above us in the distance were the snowcapped mountains in Grand Teton National Park. They were so high they were wrapped in a light mist that literally made them look purple. (*Wait, the lyrics to the song are true?*) The next few hours we drove past boiling mud pits, walked to thundering waterfalls, and wandered past steaming pools of water.

I was so grateful that my dad had invited me to look up, to get out of my own story and see the beauty of what God had created—and by extension see who God is. He had invited me into the wonder of worship.

Worship is looking up and seeing something bigger and more beautiful than just ourselves and our own stories. In moments of worship, we glimpse who God really is and our hearts become overwhelmed with wonder and praise. I used to think that God was selfish because he wanted us to worship him. But I've come to see that the call to worship is an invitation to look up and be flooded with the beauty of who God is. Our hearts open in awe of what he has done, and worship naturally pours out of us. Worship cannot be helped when we realize "in him we live and move and have our being" (Acts 17:28). Understanding with the heart transforms us entirely.

As humans we are prone to forgetfulness. (Just ask my husband. If I could, I'd put an AirTag on everything.) But worse than forgetting where we put our stuff, we forget to "look up," and that causes us to lose the hope and joy that is promised in Christ! We see people falling into forgetfulness throughout Scripture. But alongside this, we also see a gracious God who continually invites us to see his goodness and provision. Psalm 95 demonstrates how God gently tends us by guiding us back into praise when we've lost sight of him. This psalm calls us to worship, and then it pauses to remind us of a time when God's people had forgotten his faithful provision and had become stuck in their own self-interest.

Psalm 95:8-9 speaks of how the children of Israel hardened their hearts at a place called Meribah, also known as Massah, and complained to Moses because they were thirsty and had nothing to drink. In all their grumbling, they forgot that God had always provided for them. They had seen the incredible work of God in freeing them from slavery in Egypt and knew he was trustworthy. God had sent ten plagues upon Egypt because Pharaoh had enslaved the Israelites and wouldn't let them go. God's people watched as Pharaoh repeatedly declared he would release them. Then God was merciful and took away the punishment. But when pressed to follow through, Pharaoh hardened his heart again and would not let them go.

The plagues culminated in the death of the firstborn sons of the Egyptians, and at last Israel was free to leave Egypt. God himself guided them with a pillar of fire by night and a pillar of cloud by day. When Pharaoh again attempted to take them captive, God literally opened the sea in front of them so they could walk through on dry ground. They had the most powerful protection they could hope for.

Yet, much like I do when things get hard, Israel forgot they had a God who was strong and able to defend them. They built idols to other gods and refused to live in the land God had prepared for them because they were afraid of the giants that lived there (Exodus 32:1; Numbers 13:32). They were so absorbed in their day-to-day needs and wants that they forgot they had a God who had proven he was able to care for them.

We do this when we lie awake until two in the morning trying to think our way out of a problem. Sometimes we attempt to manipulate other people into reconciling rather than trusting the Holy Spirit to guide them. Or we yell at our teens or give them the silent treatment to push them into making what we think is the "right decision."

If you are a believer, God has worked powerfully in your own life. He has chased you down, redeemed you, called you by name, and restored you to his family. He has also given us an entire book that reveals who he is and tells the story of his creativity, love, and rescue. As you pause and "look up," reflecting on who he is and the things he has done, you will be led to trust and worship. You can remember his faithfulness in your own life and trust that he will be faithful in the lives of your loved ones.

God is at work in our lives each day, and when we take time to focus on who he is and what his work looks like, we are better able to see his hand in our lives. As we realize what God has done, we are moved to doxology, just as we see in the lives of God's people throughout Scripture (Romans 11:33).

God doesn't leave you to muster trust and remembrance of him all on your own, though. You are invited into worship through practical ways of remembering, such as singing songs, reading his Word, and hearing testimonies of his work in the lives of others. These practices guided both the Israelites and the New Testament church into worship for millennia. When we focus on God's faithfulness throughout the generations, we are reminded of the ways he has worked in our own lives.

The verses we are studying today, Psalm 95:6-7, are an example of the beautiful template of worship provided in the Psalms. Many psalms were intended to be sung. We are often explicitly commanded to "sing unto the Lord." There are also many physical postures mentioned throughout the Bible in connection to worship. Some of these postures include lying, standing, kneeling, lifting hands, clapping, lifting the head, bowing the head, and dancing. These are outward postures of what is happening in our hearts. We've learned through neuroscience that what we do with our bodies affects our memories and emotions as well. Our bodies matter in worship.

So purposely move into an activity that causes you to worship today. You could turn on God-glorifying music, write down the things he's done for you, call a friend and tell her something God has done in your life, or kneel by your bed and pray. Don't do these things to force feelings of praise but rather as an outpouring of the awe in your heart. When you "look up" and focus on the work Christ has done, you will engage your heart, soul, and mind in remembering his goodness, which allows your body to relax into trusting him. As you adopt a posture of worship, you will be better able to see his work in your life.

In Context

I've listed some of my favorite passages on worship below. After reading each passage in your Bible, use the space provided to respond to one (or both) of these questions:

What does this teach you about how and why to worship?

What does this reveal to you about who God is?

You can also choose to simply write out the passage. Writing the Word of God helps solidify it in our hearts.

John 4:24

Psalm 150:6

Isaiah 25:1

Psalm 71:8

A Gentle Invitation into Worship

How do you feel cared for by God today? How might that lead you into worship?

How would having a heart of worship change your daily life?

Prayer

Lord, if I take even a couple of minutes to skim through the Bible or review my life, there are so many amazing things that you have done. Usually I'm so worried about what comes next that I forget to remember what you've already done. Thank you for reminding me of your beautiful works. Help me to remember your works more often and place myself in the way of worship.

Digging Deeper into Worship

If you have bonus time, I invite you to explore an additional verse on worship. Write out Exodus 15:11 on an index card or Post-it so you can refer to it throughout your week.

> Now let's take some time to look deeply at Exodus 15:11. We want to see this verse in its context, understand the words used, and discover its meaning.

This verse is part of a song to the Lord. Can you tell from memory or by skimming the chapter who is singing this song and when?

LORD, who is like you
  among the gods?
Who is like you, glorious
  in holiness,
revered with praises,
  performing wonders?

EXODUS 15:11

List the attributes of God that are praised in this verse.

What about this song of praise makes you confused or curious?

A SECOND LOOK AT

Worship

Hearts still pounding in terror, the people of Israel turned to watch as the Red Sea thundered closed behind them.

The night before, they had camped comfortably on the other side of the sea, resting and reveling in the fact that God had rescued them from slavery in Egypt. Meanwhile, Pharaoh was tormented by the insanity of his decision to release thousands of slaves from Egypt's workforce, and he decided to chase them down with over six hundred chariots to force them to return. But God again revealed the power of his protection. He moved his presence, appearing as a pillar of fire behind the Israelites, blocking them from the view of the Egyptian army, and then he opened the sea in front of them. The Israelites could then walk across on—wait for it—*dry* ground!

Moments ago, the Egyptian army had been chasing them through the bed of the Red Sea, but now, as the people turned to look, the waves were crashing down upon the enslaving army. Not even one of them remained.

The Israelites' wonder at the work of the Lord was so overwhelming that all the people sang a song to the Lord. When we see the mighty work of God, we can't help but, in awe, break out into praise.

Worship is the human response to the work God does in our hearts through his Spirit. It can be awe experienced alone when we remember the greatness of God, but it also is a practice we observe in community with other believers. The pull of our emotions and the longing of our hearts as we move into awe is also worship.

But before we can enter into worship, we need to remember to "look up" at the goodness of God instead of focusing inward on ourselves. It's easy to lose sight of worship in the distraction and busyness of days full of work that leave us overwhelmed and exhausted. Headline after headline reminds us of how powerless we are to make big changes in the world. We become stuck in our heads over relational problems that we can't seem to overcome.

Deep down, we believe we must solve our own problems and those of others. We think everything rests on us. As time passes, we begin to crack under that pressure. When we ruminate on our own needs, wants, problems, and accomplishments, we get sucked into the vortex of self-importance. We begin to think that everything we experience is ultimate. Eventually our thoughts become so disordered that we believe we are the main character of the world. We continue on, oblivious to the way it's harming our lives and relationships.

Thank goodness God doesn't leave us there. He reminds us to look up at something bigger than ourselves. The Israelites had a front-row seat to God's saving hand as he poured the Red Sea on the ones seeking to destroy them, and it moved them to worship.

Generations later there was another flood of punishment. But this time, instead of consuming many it would be unleashed on one. Instead of being poured onto evil pursuers it would be poured onto the one who had done no wrong yet took all the punishment of the world onto himself. Just as the Israelites were moved into rejoicing for the salvation of their bodies, so, too, we are moved to overwhelming worship by the resurrection of Christ and his victory over sin and death for the saving of our souls.

Sometimes worship happens unexpectedly. A lens shifts, and we think about a Bible verse in a new way. Or a song comes on the radio and a line hits us like it hasn't before. But more often, we need to be led into worship. We have to get out of our heads and look up instead of focusing on our own stories.

We do this by intentionally placing ourselves in spaces where we know worship is found. We open our Bibles and read what God has done. We carve out time to go to church, where we sing about God's goodness together and then listen to a pastor teach on the work of God and its significance for us. Worship can't be manipulated, but there are things we can do to place ourselves in its way.

Seeing God in all his perfection also reminds us of our own guilt. You might wonder why these guilty feelings wouldn't cause us to avoid worship at all costs. But seeing the way God beautifully weaves his story of redemption throughout history leads us to see our guilt in the light of his grace. When we experience this, we immediately know his comfort. That relief leads to even more worship.

And so we intentionally move into worship—not to manipulate ourselves into feeling or to prove we are great Christians, but rather to engage our hearts, souls, and minds in the rest that comes from remembering the work Christ has done.

Don't define worship too narrowly. Everything in your life that causes you to see and remember Jesus' work can be worship. Praise is to be built into our lives (Hebrews 13:15). Every other element of the spiritual life we've been learning about in this study is meant to lead to worship. If prayer, Bible study, simplicity, or solitude makes us rejoice in *our* good works, we have moved into idolatry. This leads to the weariness that Jesus called us from when he said, "Come to me, all of you who are weary and burdened, and I will give you rest" (Matthew 11:28). But when those same practices move us into gazing on the goodness of God, we find worship in all of them.

This week, notice the things that lead your heart to worship. Maybe during a sermon the pastor calls you to remember who Jesus is. Or you may be led to worship as you recite the story of Scripture while singing along with a song on your playlist or on the radio. Tell and hear the stories of the way God has worked in your life. While out to coffee, listen to a friend share about their week and marvel at what Jesus has done.

Additional Context

I've listed some more of my favorite passages on worship below. After reading each passage in your Bible, use the space provided to respond to one (or both) of these questions:

What does this teach you about how and why to worship?

What does this reveal to you about who God is?

You can also choose to simply write out the passage. Writing the Word of God helps solidify it in our hearts.

1 Chronicles 16:34

Hebrews 13:15

Romans 12:1-2

Hebrews 12:28

A Second Invitation into Worship

What are some ways you can intentionally place yourself in the way of worship this week?

Journal about a time God showed up unexpectedly in your life and moved you to worship.

Celebration

We are told hundreds of times in the Bible to be glad and rejoice. That's not just because we love a good party. We were created to celebrate God's goodness each day. Our celebration here on earth points to the perfect feasting that we will enjoy for eternity with Jesus.

Video Notes

DISCUSSION AND REFLECTION QUESTIONS

- How have you seen important moments celebrated?
- What makes celebration hard?
- Can you think of a time when someone celebrated you well?

To access the video session, use the instructions in the front of your Bible study book.

A Record of God's Gentle Tending

Sometimes we think God doesn't meet with us, when really we just don't pause long enough to notice what he's already doing. Take a moment to record how God is tending you.

Record a time when you celebrated an important event in your life or the life of a loved one. How did you celebrate, and who was involved? What brought feelings of joy and excitement?

Finding Celebration in the Word

Write out Philippians 4:4 on an index card or Post-it so you can refer to it throughout your week.

> Now let's take some time to look deeply at Philippians 4:4. We want to see this verse in its context, understand the words used, and discover its meaning.

What is the repeated instruction in this verse?

Rejoice in the Lord always. I will say it again: Rejoice!

PHILIPPIANS 4:4

Why do you think we have to be told to rejoice? In what ways might rejoicing be countercultural?

This verse was written by the apostle Paul. What aspects of Paul's life could have made it difficult for him to put this verse into practice? (If you can't think of an example, see 2 Corinthians 11:24-25.)

LET'S DIG INTO

Celebration

One Sunday I looked through our church bulletin and realized that all the events listed for that week were either work or meetings. We were so good at taking meals to people after a family member passed. Finding volunteers to show up to do work in the churchyard was easy. Women immediately wrote and sent cards when someone was sick, and our pastor was great at going to the hospital to visit people.

But other than hosting baby showers and decorating the church for Christmas, we didn't show up to celebrate one another at all. This lack of celebration stood out to me even more because I had just listened to a podcast in which the host grieved the fact that as adults we quit celebrating one another and being celebrated. We reach huge milestones, sigh, and move on to work on the next thing.

That night I journaled, "That's it. This ends with me. I'm going to start intentionally celebrating milestones. I'm going to write my own celebrations down. I'm going to ask people to celebrate with me. I'm going to take people out for their birthdays. I'm going to listen for big moments in the lives of others and note them. I'm going to make feasts and celebrate more than a hobbit from the Shire."

I did pretty well at celebrating for a while, but then life happened and I fell out of the new habits I'd created. Even so, God wouldn't let me completely abandon what he'd placed on my heart. A couple of years later, the urge to celebrate started itching for reclamation.

In a podcast interview I did with Jen Wilkin, she pointed out that as humans, we tend to think we own time.[31] This shows up in two opposite ways. The first is that we fill our schedules and optimize all our free time. We think that if we just show up in the right way, we will accomplish everything we want to do. The second is that we put everything off until another day. We believe we will always have more than enough time.

I think these false beliefs that sabotage life also sabotage our celebrations. We believe we can't pause to celebrate because we must reach for the next milestone, or we believe we will have time to celebrate later. In both instances, we fall into the trap of believing we are without end. But when we "number our days carefully" (Psalm 90:12), remembering that our time on earth is limited, we are better positioned to appreciate each present moment and rejoice in our eternal hope.

Celebration is a deeply Christian practice. We kick off the story of Jesus' birth with a host of angels crying out in song, "Glory to God in the highest heaven, and peace on earth to people he favors!" (Luke 2:14). And before returning to heaven, Jesus declared to his disciples, "I have told you these things so that my joy may be in you and your joy may be complete" (John 15:11).

The Bible tells us often to be glad and rejoice. Not just because a good party is fun, but because we were created to celebrate God's goodness each day. He created us, our world, and all that is in it. Even though sin has marred the world, there is so much beauty to behold. The celebrations we enjoy today point to the perfect feasting and celebration found in eternity with Jesus.

Jesus came to bring the Year of Jubilee (Luke 4:18-19). In the Old Testament, the Year of Jubilee was part of the law of Moses. It was a time to celebrate not only that God had brought the Israelites out of Egypt, but that he had promised to come again. As part of the celebration, they were to cancel all debts, a nod to the debt that Jesus would pay for them. They were to release slaves as they had been released. No crops were to be planted, a reminder that God feeds and provides for his people. And property purchased was to be returned to the original inheritor. This was countercultural to the nations around them, who enslaved their own countrymen and used the financial hard times of others to amass wealth for themselves. The Year of Jubilee was intended to remind God's people that this earth wasn't their home, and they were all coheirs bound for the new Kingdom.

The Israelites were to celebrate the provision of a gracious God. He had proved he would provide for them, so they didn't need to accumulate or hoard resources. They were given an opportunity for perfect freedom from anxiety and worry. That is basis for celebration. We know God cares for us, so we can cast all our burdens on him.

But never in Scripture do we read that Israel ever observed the Year of Jubilee. Like many things in the Old Testament law, it was too high a standard to be met through human effort and served to reveal why we need a Savior.

Jesus came to bring us the ultimate Year of Jubilee—not only to challenge the unjust social and economic systems of this world but to produce internal, spiritual change in us as well. We can celebrate with joy because he paid for us to have eternal life in his Kingdom, where we will have everything we need. We can live with unbridled joy because he promises that we have everything we need for "life and godliness" (2 Peter 1:3).

The Bible lays out the beautiful story of God's plan for human flourishing that starts in the Old Testament and is made clearer in the New Testament. Even though humans sinned, introducing brokenness into the world, God continually reached out with mercy and grace to bring us back into right relationship with him. Jesus came to pay the ultimate price and rescue us from the misery of sin, pain, and the "thorns" that curse the ground (Genesis 3:18). Because of his sacrifice, we now live with the hope that one day he will bring us into a new Kingdom of no more tears, full of flourishing and joy. God uses the ordinary things already in our lives to show us what true Kingdom joy can look like, if only we will look for it.

God is so serious about celebration and joy that he commanded us to regularly celebrate when we gather and share the bread and wine of Communion (Luke 22:19). When we celebrate, we are to remember what Jesus has done and what he's going to do. We literally "taste and see that the LORD is good" (Psalm 34:8). We find joy in remembering what God has done. These are places where lasting joy comes to live, the kind of joy with no hangovers.

You can be gently tended into joy by recognizing even the small things God has done for you. This week, consider taking a photo of one thing that brings you joy each day. Or make a list of your friends' birthdays and then bring a bouquet of flowers to them on their special day or ask them over for a small dinner.

Next time you reach the end of a project, invite a few friends to go out with you to celebrate over dinner. It can feel weird to ask people to celebrate something good in your life, but as you plan, remember that marking milestones for a believer isn't about self-centered ego. Rather, it's about celebrating the faithfulness of God in your life. You don't have to feel weird about calling people together because you are reflecting on what God has done and the way that he has invited you into his work. In this way, you will be following Paul's encouragement in Philippians 4:4 to "rejoice in the Lord always," celebrating your Savior in every moment of life.

In Context

I've listed some of my favorite passages on celebration below. After reading each passage in your Bible, use the space provided to respond to one (or both) of these questions:

What does this teach you about how and why to celebrate?

What does this reveal to you about who God is?

You can also choose to simply write out the passage. Writing the Word of God helps solidify it in our hearts.

Ecclesiastes 3:1-4

Colossians 2:16-17

Luke 15:23-24

1 Corinthians 10:31

A Gentle Invitation into Celebration

What makes it hard to celebrate?

What is one way you could move into celebration this week?

Prayer

Lord, you have given us so many good gifts and made us with the capacity—and even the need—for joy. I often neglect celebration and joy in favor of easy dopamine hits or the next project. Thank you for inviting me into the kind of joy that expands and never ends. Help me to seek out opportunities to celebrate and invite others to join me!

Digging Deeper into Celebration

If you have bonus time, I invite you to explore an additional verse on celebration. Write out Psalm 118:24 on an index card or Post-it so you can refer to it throughout your week.

Now let's take some time to look deeply at Psalm 118:24. We want to see this verse in its context, understand the words used, and discover its meaning.

According to this verse, what is our basis for joy in each day?

This is the day the LORD has
made;
let's rejoice and be glad in it.
PSALM 118:24

What are the key words in this verse? How would you define them? What are the dictionary definitions?

How would you express the idea of this passage in your own words?

A SECOND LOOK AT

Celebration

In our family, on "Friday Movie Nights" my husband and I play some of our favorite childhood movies for our kids. One of my favorites is the 1960 Disney classic *Pollyanna*. It just so happened that while I was writing this book, we watched it together.

Both my husband and I grew up with this movie, and the part that stuck with us was the comically fierce pastor preaching, "Death comes unexpectedly!" while he navigates corrupt small-town politics.

But as we watched it again as adults, we were both struck by the beautiful way Pollyanna infused joy into everyday situations through little acts of kindness. She delighted in small things, causing others to see the beauty of them too. Simple acts of kindness changed the course of a day.

Toward the end of the movie, Pollyanna winsomely tells the fierce pastor that her father, also a pastor, recited a quote by Abraham Lincoln when he was feeling discouraged: "When you look for the bad in mankind, expecting to find it, you surely will." Then she said after her father found that quote, he invited her to join him as he searched through the Bible for what they called the "glad passages"—verses like "shout for joy" and "be glad in the Lord." She declares happily that they found eight hundred happy texts!

Quietly she concludes, "If God took the trouble to tell us eight hundred times to be glad and rejoice, he must have wanted us to do it."[32]

My husband and I glanced at each other as the scene closed. It hit deeply. When we were kids, the wonder of the world was easy to see. Somehow in the transformation to adulthood it takes more to impress us. Maybe that's part of why we are called to have the faith of a child (see Matthew 18:3-4).

Today's verse, Psalm 118:24, tells us to rejoice in "the day the Lord has made." This verse comes at the end of a group of psalms that were traditionally recited during Passover. In previous sessions, we discussed how Israel had been enslaved for hundreds of years in Egypt. In Exodus 3 it says that God heard the cry of his people, and then he sent Moses to tell Pharaoh to release his people. When Pharaoh refused, God used plagues to display his power and destroy the power Egypt until finally the slaves walked out free.

The final plague was the death of all the firstborn sons of Egypt. That should call our attention back to Exodus 1, when the Egyptians had demanded that all the sons of Israel be thrown into the Nile. God supernaturally spared Moses, and now he was declaring freedom for all Israel.

Psalm 118 celebrates the anniversary of Israel's freedom. They were oppressed, and everything looked like it was lost, yet the day of rescue that the Lord had planned came at last. They rejoiced in this day of salvation and were glad in it.

We can only celebrate well if we understand what we are saved from. The Israelites had experienced death, bondage, and a life dedicated to building the empire of another nation. If we take a look at our lives before salvation, we see that we are saved from the same things. Death and bondage are all around us. Sometimes it's the actual death of loved ones; other times it's chronic illness that exhausts us and reminds us of our mortality. People we love wrestle with addiction and are unable to escape its clutches. We see parents who spend all their time amassing wealth but overlook the souls of their children. The Israelites lived in physical bondage, and without Jesus we are living in painful slavery to sin.

God didn't take our firstborn children to wake us up to our condition, though. Instead, he offered up his own Son to die on the cross. Jesus was taken in ultimate bondage and nailed to the cross. The sky became dark and God refused the cries of his own Son. Christ took on bondage, breaking it once and for all, that we might find complete freedom. *This is the day the Lord has made! Let's rejoice and be glad in it!*

Celebration is the antidote to the sadness of sin that oppresses our hearts daily. We cry, "These things shouldn't be" and "This isn't the way it will be forever." It can be easy to sink into depression when we consider the state of the world and the way sin has marred it. Yet when we gather with other believers to celebrate the work God has already done and is doing, we find reason for much joy, even in a broken world.

Seeing how God has worked through time and history keeps us from dramatizing our current issues to a monumental level. It can be tempting to believe the lies of our own age, such as, "Things have never been worse in the world" or "Culture is going downhill at an unprecedented rate. Anyone who can't see it must have their eyes closed."

But the truth is, we live in *a* time and *a* place. As we dig into the Bible and see the sins of people in other times and places, we can view our current problems and pains with the right level of urgency. We can step out of the spiral of exaggeration and allow ourselves joy. "Those who look to him are radiant with joy" (Psalm 34:5).

Maybe you're exhausted from caring for others. How can you be gently tended into joy and celebration when your energy is low? As grown-ups we often turn celebration into a competitive and consumeristic activity with plastic streamers and dedicated social media posts. So what does true celebration look like? I think this is where the "faith of a child" might help us out. Let's look at how kids celebrate. Most of these take zero time and energy, so it will be easy to pick one to start with today! (Remember that kids celebrate with lots of breaks for naps, snacks, and cuddles, so intersperse accordingly.)

- **Sing.** My kids sing to themselves nearly every waking minute. My husband and I laughed just this week because we could hear happy humming even at 9:00 p.m. as they were falling asleep. You don't have to be classically trained to find joy in song. Psalm 100:1 invites all of us to "make a joyful noise to the Lord" (ESV). So turn some music up and celebrate.
- **Laugh in delight.** *Psychology Today* highlighted that the average four-year-old laughs about three hundred times a day and the average forty-year-old laughs only four times a day![33] Place yourself in the way of laughter. Watch something funny or go find a four-year-old and join in the delight.
- **Share good stories.** If something good happens to a small child—even if it's a little thing—everyone around them is going to hear about it . . . at length. We can tend to get embarrassed about sharing our joy with others. Be the person others can share their joy with and find one joy-filled thing to share with others too.

- **Dance around.** Little kids love to dance. We also see dancing throughout Scripture, such as when David danced before the Lord (2 Samuel 6:14, 16) and Miriam, along with all the Israelite women, danced after the Red Sea rescue (Exodus 15:20). I am undeniably awful at dancing, but watching my youngest son dance and wiggle around when he's full of delight is so inspiring. Maybe we can work on folding this one into our lives together.
- **Find joy in play.** I once showed up to our neighbor's house with a pack of stickers for their kids. You would have thought I'd brought them the crown jewels. The delight and squeals of joy for a two-dollar pack of stickers still makes me smile when I think of it twenty years later. Kids often find joy in the simple things of life, and we can too. So pick flowers. Design homemade cards. Read or write a poem. Tell a joke. Set up a date where you invite friends over for handicrafts or to paint.
- **Eat with people!** Kids love to be celebrated with food. When they are invited to help make their birthday cake, pick what's for dinner, or even go out for burgers, it makes them absolutely glowy. They embrace it without the self-consciousness that comes through adult experiences. Build a culture of celebration into your friend group. Celebrate finishing a major project, milestone, or a new job by eating a special meal.

You are created in the image of a God of joy, which means you find wholeness in joy. As you remember who he is and what he has done this week, hold on to his promise that "in [his] presence is abundant joy" (Psalm 16:11).

Additional Context

I've listed some more of my favorite passages on celebration below. After reading each passage in your Bible, use the space provided to respond to one (or both) of these questions:

What does this teach you about how and why to celebrate?

What does this reveal to you about who God is?

You can also choose to simply write out the passage. Writing the Word of God helps solidify it in our hearts.

Psalm 95:2

1 Corinthians 5:8

Ecclesiastes 2:24-25

Luke 15:3-10

A Second Invitation into Celebration

What is a day that God "made for you," where you can see that he planned for your rescue in advance? How might you celebrate the ways he faithfully provided for you?

How are you feeling called into celebration today?

Conclusion

More than anything else, as we close this study what I hope you take away is that you don't need to practice these twelve spiritual disciplines to make God love you more. God already loves you intimately and so deeply that he gave up his own life to restore your relationship with him. Today he's already beside you, he feels both the joy and pain that touches your heart, he wants to gently tend you, and he is inviting you to experience his nearness through the spiritual disciplines he's provided.

My deepest prayer as I have written these words is that this isn't the end of your journey, but rather the beginning. I hope that the awareness of God's presence that you have felt and the things that you have learned cause you to continue to study his Word one verse at a time, turning your ordinary minutes into moments with God.

The Bible says that as you know and love God through the practices of the spiritual disciplines, you will be transformed to look more like him. Even on days you're overwhelmed, you will be able to show up with more love, joy, peace, patience, kindness, goodness, faithfulness, gentleness, and self-control than you ever thought you were capable of.

Leader's Guide

A Note to the Leader on Gently Tending

The goal of this study is to invite you into the gentle tending of Jesus in every moment. As the group leader, you play an important role in fostering a space where the women in your group can feel their Savior's care for them in community. The good news is, because God is gently tending each of you, you don't have to worry about getting all the theological answers right or carry the responsibility of fixing everyone's problems. This frees you to be a loving presence as you look to God for answers together.

Scripture tells us, "He protects his flock like a shepherd; he gathers the lambs in his arms and carries them in the fold of his garment. He gently leads those that are nursing" (Isaiah 40:11). God cares about the weakness of his flock and provides soothing, comfortable arrangements for those who are feeling overwhelmed. Your humanity and the humanity of the people who attend your class is not a surprise to God. He longs to gently tend you exactly where you are.

Before you begin this Bible study, consider what your group has capacity for. You can choose to make this a three-, six-, or twelve-week study. You might cover four disciplines each week, or perhaps you have space for just one or two disciplines per week. No matter where your group lands, remember that every moment given to God—no matter how big or small—will produce transformation in your life.

As you lead, I hope you will focus on caring deeply for the people in your group and not feel pressured to impress others with what you know. To paraphrase Maya Angelou, people often don't remember what you say, but they do remember how you made them feel. Ask God to help you lead your group with gentleness, humility, and love.

In the pages that follow, I've provided some helpful tips for guiding your group through the *Gently Tended* Bible study.

Comforts

Before group members arrive, take some time to create a warm, welcoming space for study. Some ways I like to do this include lighting a candle, turning on some soft background music, or setting out tea or a snack. When I incorporate these small comforts into my Bible studies, I find that it slows my own heart, helping me step away from the hustle and be present with the other women who attend. It doesn't have to be fancy, expensive, or time-consuming to be intentional.

Opening Prayer

After everyone has arrived and had a few minutes to connect and get a snack or something to drink, kick things off by praying and inviting God to tend your souls.

Starting Things Off

A good question to begin with is "What stood out to you from the reading this week?" This allows group members who read and did all the homework to share what they learned. It also catches people up who may not have had time to get to the reading.

Following this up with the short video teaching that introduces the spiritual discipline, and then the discussion questions provided in the book, will allow all members to contribute. After this, you can invite group members to open up their Bibles, read the session's focus verse, and share their answers to the questions provided in each lesson.

Asking Good Questions

Ask a variety of questions to get the group talking. You can pull some from the study or ask ones you feel the Lord leading you toward. As the leader, less is more when it comes to talking. As you share and answer, lead with humility and vulnerability, but lean into silence and group participation over monologue. The Holy Spirit is there to teach and lead. You don't have to feel responsible to answer everyone's questions. Listening and empathy yield the best group conversations.

When fostering discussion in Bible study, I like to use the same method my boys use at school for group discussion:

- *I notice . . .* (Share your observations!)
- *I wonder . . .* (What are you curious about?)
- *This reminds me of . . .* (Connect the text to your personal experience or other verses and stories from Scripture.)

You may see echoes of this in the questions I've written into your study, but you may also want to use these prompts directly to get even more out of your study. Other questions and prompts you can use include the following:

- I'll start by sharing my favorite quote. Then I'd love for you to share yours!
- What did you underline from your reading?
- What surprised you about this verse?
- What key words stood out?
- What did you learn about God's character from studying this discipline?
- What is one bit of this Scripture you've applied to an aspect of your life this week? What did that show you?
- How might today's lesson change the way you live, work, suffer, parent, etc., this coming week?

Troubleshooting

If you notice that one or two people are doing all the talking, you might find it helpful to use the "Three Then Me" rule for discussion: After someone speaks, they let three other people share their thoughts before speaking again. This helps make space for quieter members of the group and prevents any one person from dominating the conversation. Feel free to state this each week as a reminder to allow everyone's voice to be heard.

Allowing Room for Silence

As the leader, don't feel pressured to fill all the gaps in conversation. Silence allows group members to process what they're learning and respond thoughtfully. It's especially helpful for those who may need more time to formulate their ideas. While you don't want to pause for too long, a healthy amount of silence can deepen the conversation and encourage greater group participation.

Closing Prayer

As you close each session in prayer, remind your group that prayer isn't public speaking to God. This isn't the time to preach a mini sermon at the end of the lesson or show how many church words you know. Prayer is how we enter into the gentle tending of God. He greets the prayers of your group with the open, loving arms of a father. You can run to him with the joy and pain of your daily life. Ultimately, your goal is for every group member's faith to be deepened.

A Final Thank-You

Thank you for choosing to lead the women in your group through this *Gently Tended* Bible study. Leaders like you have helped me through difficult spiritual seasons. I know that leading a study is a sacrifice. I pray that as you take time to care for and disciple others amid the busyness of life, you will feel the gentle tending of your Savior each moment and be refreshed as you enter into deeper relationship with him.

Elizabeth

Acknowledgments

I was having coffee with my experienced author friend Asheritah when, like the weirdo I am, I blurted out, "How do you engage with all the books you're reading for research while writing a book on a similar topic?"

She paused thoughtfully and replied, "I like to imagine I'm sitting at a table in conversation with all the saints who have gone before me. I listen to them discuss for a long time, and then I chime in with what I have learned about who God is through my own walk with him."

I took that with me into this whole process.

Throughout this study you've seen the names of saints who sat at my table to counsel me through their writings. Below are the others who have not come to the table in book form but have been at my table counseling and encouraging me along the way.

To my husband, who kept me from giving up years ago when I first started writing. He took over work I usually do to make space for it and poured over the pages of writing, giving insights, and brainstorming better ways to phrase things.

To Keaton, Cedric, and Keller, who know how to help me celebrate all the little steps in this book. If it weren't for you, I wouldn't know the delight of God in the way I've come to love. And to Nei, who took my little ones in her own arms to free my hands for writing and a different kind of Kingdom work.

To my parents, who saturated me in God's Word, guiding me to memorize hundreds of verses, many chapters, and entire books of the Bible.

Thank you, Ashley Hales, for telling me it was time to try to write a book and then starting introductions the same day. Thank you for listening to my joy and tears through this process and encouraging me to persevere.

Thank you, Caroline Saunders and Abbey Wedgeworth, for your hours guiding me through the beginnings of the publishing process and being available for questions and curiosities.

To my pastors and the spiritual directors of my church, Chad Kinser, Brian and Myrna Elliot, Dillon Byrd, and Leslie Poe, who prayed for this project, equipped me to write through book recommendations, and helped me to grow as a teacher.

Thank you to my agent, Andrew Wolgemuth, for listening to my wild idea of a different kind of Bible study. The way you went to bat for this idea humbled me to tears more than once. Your faithfulness to steward words not yet written is beautiful Kingdom work.

To Kara Leonino for taking the time to come see me and practically map out what each page needed to look like to make a vague idea become reality. To Elizabeth Czajkowski for asking good questions and posing perspectives and thoughts that made me level everything up.

I'm so grateful for the seasoned women of faith—Ting, Nancy, Bennye, Cindy, Carolyn, Cindy, and Dee—who have taught me to study the Bible. They cut up the meat and put it on my plate when I was too tired for steak but wanted more than milk. And for Danae, who slipped that first pack of index cards into my hands.

I'm so grateful to Cassandra Speer, Joanna Kimbrel, Courtney Doctor, Karen Hodge, Katie Orr, and Jen Oshman, who have published books ahead of me, advised me, and pulled me along toward this project.

No project would be completed without its cheerleaders, and God has abundantly blessed me with Anna, Holly, Chelsi, Emily, Ursula, Caitlyn, Morgan, Joy, Sally, Megan, Ashlee, and Stephanie.

Notes

1. Dietrich Bonhoeffer, *Life Together* (Harper and Row, 1954), 83.

2. Jen Wilkin, *Women of the Word: How to Study the Bible with Both Our Hearts and Our Minds* (Crossway, 2014), 31.

3. For more on ancient Rome, see Dominic Wilkinson, "Exposure and Infanticide in Ancient Rome," *Death or Disability? The 'Carmentis Machine' and Decision-Making for Critically Ill Children* (Oxford University Press, 2013), https://doi.org/10.1093/acprof:oso/9780199669431.003.0008; Shelia Cadge, "Roman Women and Reproduction, Part 4: Childhood," Vindolanda Charitable Trust, accessed November 20, 2025, https://www.vindolanda.com/blog/roman-women-and-children-part-4; PBS.org, "Women," The Roman Empire in the First Century, accessed November 20, 2025, https://www.pbs.org/empires/romans/empire/women.html; Only Bilal Writes, "Gladiators Games: Ancient Rome's Deadly Entertainment," Medium, November 27, 2024, https://onlybilalwrites.medium.com/gladiators-games-ancient-romes-deadly-entertainment-f9c1263e0070.

4. Justin B., host, *Stories of the Called*, podcast, season 1, episode 9, "Darlene Deibler Rose," Apple Podcasts, January 1, 2025, https://podcasts.apple.com/sg/podcast/darlene-deibler-rose-ep-9/id1776500670?i=1000682473853.

5. For more on "Praying Hyde," see Richard Klein, "Profiles in Prayer: Praying John Hyde," The Christian Broadcasting Network, https://cbn.com/article/not-selected/profiles-prayer-praying-john-hyde-0.

6. Michael Reeves, *Enjoy Your Prayer Life* (10Publishing, 2014), 36–37.

7. "Don't Worry, Be Thankful: Eucharisteo with Ann Voskamp," Theology of Work (blog), accessed October 24, 2025, https://www.theologyofwork.org/the-high-calling/dont-worry-be-thankful-eucharisteo-ann-voskamp/.

8. Johnson Oatman, "Count Your Blessings," Hymnary.org, accessed September 29, 2025, https://hymnary.org/text/when_upon_lifes_billows_you_are_tempest.

9. "In His Own Words—Time of Thanksgiving," The Billy Graham Library, November 27, 2014, https://billygrahamlibrary.org/in-his-own-words-time-of-thanksgiving/.

10. Bonhoeffer, *Life Together*, 83.

11. Jesse Corti and Richard White, vocalists, "Gaston," by Alan Menken and Howard Ashman, track 4 on *Beauty and the Beast: Original Motion Picture Soundtrack*, Walt Disney Records, 1991, https://www.youtube.com/watch?v=pC7aPpY6jPQ.

12. "This World Is Not My Home," Timeless Truths, accessed November 20, 2025, https://library.timelesstruths.org/music/This_World_Is_Not_My_Home/.

13. Quoted from "You Are My Sunshine," performed by Jimmie Davis with Charles Mitchell's Orchestra, produced by Jimmie Davis and Charles Mitchell, Decca, 1940, https://www.youtube.com/watch?v=Hzh8EZ-bPJc.

14. "Philippians 2:6-11—The Christ Hymn of Philippians," Enter the Bible, accessed October 27, 2025, https://enterthebible.org/passage/philippians-26-11-the-christ-hymn-of-philippians.

15. For more on this concept, see Richard J. Foster, *Celebration of Discipline: The Path to Spiritual Growth* (HarperSanFrancisco, 1988), 110–111.

16. See Timothy Keller, *The Freedom of Self-Forgetfulness: The Path to True Christian Joy* (10Publishing, 2012).

17. See Rick Warren, *The Purpose Driven Life: What on Earth Am I Here For?* (Zondervan, 2002), 148.

18. Adapted from Melissa Kruger's *Wherever You Go, I Want You to Know . . .* (The Good Book Company, 2020).

19. Foster, *Celebration of Discipline*, 136.

20. Foster, *Celebration of Discipline*, 132.

21. Foster, *Celebration of Discipline*, 127.

22. Adapted from Bob Flayhart's three-step "Gospel Waltz." See Bob Flayhart, Holly Mackle, *The Gospel Waltz: Experiencing the Transformational Power of Grace* (GCD Books, 2023).

23. See The Episcopal Church, *The Book of Common Prayer* (Church Publishing Incorporated, 2007), 321, https://www.episcopalchurch.org/wp-content/uploads/2023/06/book_of_common_prayer.pdf.

24. Adapted from Bob Flayhart's three-step "Gospel Waltz." See also Elizabeth Santelmann, host, *Sunshine in My Nest*, podcast, "Coping with Anger in Parenting with Bob Flayhart," Apple Podcasts, September 26, 2023, https://podcasts.apple.com/us/podcast/69-coping-with-anger-in-parenting-with-bob-flayhart/id1625483086?i=1000629181236.

25. The Episcopal Church, *The Book of Common Prayer*, 317.
26. Shivani Zoting, "Productivity Management Software Market Growth Fueled by AI and Automation," Precedence Research, last updated July 8, 2025, https://www.precedenceresearch.com/productivity-management-software-market.
27. Gustaf Wingren, *Luther on Vocation* (Muhlenberg Press, 1957), 10.
28. For more on this story, see "A Famous Story About Muller's Faith," GeorgeMuller.org, June 29, 2016, https://www.georgemuller.org/devotional/a-famous-story-about-mullers-faith.
29. Mary Oliver, "The Summer Day," *New and Selected Poems, vol. 1* (Beacon Press, 1992), 94.
30. Elizabeth Santelmann, host, *Sunshine in My Nest*, podcast, "Living Life with the End in Mind with Jen Wilkin," Apple Podcasts, May 27, 2025, https://podcasts.apple.com/ma/podcast/living-life-with-the-end-in-mind-with-jen-wilkin/id1625483086?i=1000710106629.
31. Santelmann, *Sunshine in My Nest*, "Living Life with the End in Mind."
32. *Pollyanna*, directed by David Swift (Walt Disney Productions, 1960), DVD; see also Becky Cline, "Glad Tidings: The Walt Disney Archives Finds a Lost Treasure," Walt Disney Archives, May 19, 2020, https://d23.com/glad-tidings/.
33. Pamela Gerloff, "You're Not Laughing Enough, and That's No Joke," *Psychology Today*, June 21, 2011, https://www.psychologytoday.com/us/blog/the-possibility-paradigm/201106/youre-not-laughing-enough-and-thats-no-joke.

Books at My Table

Celebration of Discipline: The Path to Spiritual Growth
by Richard Foster

The Spirit of the Disciplines: Understanding How God Changes Lives
by Dallas Willard

Enjoy Your Prayer Life
by Michael Reeves

Habits of Grace: Enjoying Jesus through the Spiritual Disciplines
by David Mathis

The Ruthless Elimination of Hurry: How to Stay Emotionally Healthy and Spiritually Alive in the Chaos of the Modern World
by John Mark Comer

Life Together: The Classic Exploration of Christian Community
by Dietrich Bonhoffer

Reclaiming Quiet: Cultivating a Life of Holy Attention
by Sarah Clarkson

Delighting in Jesus: Rhythms to Restore Joy When You Feel Burdened, Broken, or Burned-Out
by Asheritah Ciuciu

Women of the Word: How to Study the Bible with Both Our Hearts and Our Minds
by Jen Wilkin

The Practice of the Presence of God
by Brother Lawrence

The Story Retold: A Biblical-Theological Introduction to the New Testament
by G. K. Beale and Benjamin L. Gladd

Scripture Index

About the Author

Elizabeth Santelmann has been studying the Bible for thirty years. Throughout her childhood, her family encouraged the memorization of large passages of Scripture. As an adult, she attended Bible Study Fellowship (BSF) and local Bible studies based on books by Jen Wilkin and Nancy Guthrie, and she also audited seminary classes while nursing her babies.

Elizabeth was trained as a children's Bible teacher and worked for three years in children's ministry before having her own kids. She spent seven years writing and sharing on her Instagram and blog before launching her popular podcast, *Sunshine in My Nest*.

She currently lives in Oklahoma with her husband and three sons. Elizabeth is passionate about the work of her local church and serves by hosting a weekly discipleship group in her home, leading a small group in student ministry, and facilitating outreach studies periodically throughout the year.